autumn leaves

For Jake on her 50th
autumn is your time
of year. . . .
all love to you from
Nancy and Carlton
September 28, 1991

Williamsburg
Virginia

autumn leaves

A GUIDE TO THE FALL COLORS
OF THE NORTHWOODS

Ronald M. Lanner

Photography by Robert W. Baldwin
Cover Photographs by Gary Griffen

NorthWord
PRESS, INC.

FROM THE NORTHWORD
NATURE GUIDE COLLECTION

Designed by Moonlit Ink, Madison, Wisconsin
Cover photographs by Gary Griffen
Inside photographs by Robert W. Baldwin

Published By

NorthWord Press, Inc.
Box 1360
Minocqua, WI 54548

For a Free Catalog describing NorthWord's line of
nature books and gifts, call 1-800-336-5666

The quotes on pages 58 and 99 of this book are taken from *A Natural
History of Trees of Eastern and Central North America,* 2nd edition,
by Donald Culross Peattie. Copyright 1948, 1949, 1950 by Donald
Culross Peattie. Copyright © 1950 by Paul Landacre. Reprinted by
permission of Houghton Mifflin Company.

Printed in Singapore
ISBN 1-55971-078-0

*To my parents, Louis and Esther Lanner, who
first brought me to these woods.*

The area covered by *Autumn Leaves*

PREFACE

Years ago, a friend who lived on the seashore was shocked to learn that the admired scent of salt air was due in part to the odor of decomposing marine organisms. But knowing this should not detract from anyone's fun at the beach, where, after all, the sun still shines as brightly, and the waves still break into foam. Nor should it detract from our enjoyment of the woods to know that brilliant fall colors foretell the imminent wholesale death of once-green leaves preparing to go to earth and decay. It might even heighten our enjoyment of autumn, by lending a sense of urgency to the task of getting out into the country before the colors fade and the trees drop their foliage.

In recent years more people than ever have apparently felt this urgency, because autumn foliage has been attracting tourists and travelers by the millions to wooded areas of the Midwest and Northeast, especially New England, and eastern Canada. This region is home to over ninety million people, and sometimes it seems that all of them are in the woods during "leaf season," for here colormania has reached unprecedented heights. Each fall the inns are filled, buses are chartered, cars crowd the highways, and bikers and hikers hit the roads and trails, as legions of "leaf-peepers" open their eyes to nature's extravagance.

And extravagance it seems to be, because there appears to be no good reason for a tree to take on scarlet, gold, or wine. A brilliant flower can attract the pollinating insect or bird it needs for the plant's reproduction, but a brilliant leaf attracts only the gaze of its admirers.

This book is aimed at those admirers of northern fall colors, and at other outdoors people who would like to get acquainted with some of the many and varied trees of our region. It is not a comprehensive manual of northern trees; it is a selection of those that contribute most importantly to the fall brilliance across our region, including some of the evergreen conifers whose somber green serves as a foil to that brilliance. It is designed to help the reader identify the tree as seen in the fall, to sketch out something of its natural history and relationship to North American culture and to call attention to the interrelationships of our trees with other ecosystem inhabitants. Many of the trees emphasized appear with an animal likely to be found perching in it, gliding through its shade, or even eating it.

Despite its stunning photographs, this is a working book intended to be brought along on trips to the woods, for pressing leaves if nothing more. Readers who wish to use this book as a stepping stone to further information about the trees and leaves it describes will find in the back a list of references.

CONTENTS

cool fires of autumn

Being a Reasoned Explanation of Why Autumn Leaves Turn Color, With Suggestions for Pleasant and Fruitful Leaf-Peeping

THE NATURE OF COLOR

High above Planet Earth the whirring and clicking cameras of orbiting satellites record each September a change in the reflectance of sunlight by vegetation of the northern hemisphere. It is fall, and hundreds of millions of tons of chlorophyll are being destroyed, victimized by the programmed senescence of the leaves in which most chlorophyll is found.

From their summer green they have gone to a sere brown. As Robert Frost tells us in his poem *"In Hardwood Groves"*:

> *The same leaves over and over again!*
> *They fall from giving shade above*
> *To make one texture of faded brown*
> *And fit the earth like a leather glove.*

But before they fall from giving shade many of these leaves will briefly erupt in brilliant color, like flames flickering once more, brightly, then expiring.

In order to understand why and how green leaves become scarlet or golden leaves becomes dry brown leaves we must learn a little about leaves, and sugar, and pigments, and hormones, and how trees react to changing day length and temperatures.

Leaves emerge in the spring from buds formed the previous summer, having spent the winter tightly wrapped in a cover of weather-resistant bud scales. The bursting of the buds is brought about by the restless growth of the embryonic leaves within, which is in turn the consequence of warming air and soil, and lengthening days. It is the fate of a young leaf—if it survives the beaks and mandibles of insects, strong winds, hot sun, and late frosts—to fill itself with cell sap, make millions of chlorophyll molecules, and synthesize sugars that will fuel the growth and respiration of the tree.

Chlorophyll is a light-absorbing pigment found in two forms—*a* and *b*—in our trees. These differ in the compo-

(overleaf)

Red Oak leaves owe their fall coloration to anthocyanins, the same pigments that make grapes purple and apples red.

(opposite page)

Black Tupelo is a fine honey plant that enters the southern edge of our region.

sition of their molecules, but they function similarly. Chlorophyll molecules are found in tiny, green, saucer-shaped bodies called chloroplasts, where they are organized in complex layered structures. The chloroplasts are most heavily concentrated in leaf blades, but they are also found in other green tissues like flower stalks and fruits. Sometimes a rare mutation will prevent chlorophyll from forming in a plant, and a short-lived albino seedling will develop, or a more durable plant sporting variegated green-and-white leaves.

Light is essential for chlorophyll manufacture, but if it is too bright, it destroys chlorophyll. Low temperatures also destroy chlorophyll, giving many evergreen conifers a brownish winter look.

Chlorophyll's instability caused difficulties for early distributors of canned vegetables—after all, who would want to buy cans of gray peas? They soon learned, however, that if the magnesium atom at the center of the chlorophyll molecule was replaced with a copper atom, the green became permanent. This artificial "copper chlorophyll" is what we find in green toothpaste, shampoo, and food products.

The concentration of chlorophyll in leaf tissues is also affected by the tree's nutrition. If nitrogen, iron, magnesium, or some other elements are in short supply in the soil, the rate of chlorophyll formation will decline; but restoring these nutrients will increase chlorophyll production. That is why shade trees often "green up" after being fertilized. Thus the balance between synthesis of new chlorophyll and destruction of old chlorophyll is a dynamic one that changes with changing conditions in the tree's environment. When all is well, chloroplasts grow in number faster than they are broken down. Well-lighted chlorophyll molecules by the uncounted million take carbon atoms from atmospheric carbon dioxide; oxygen is returned into the air, and the resulting sugar solution becomes available for the tree's many needs.

In addition to chloroplasts, there are also chromoplasts in the leaf which contain non-photosynthetic pigments. These are the carotenoids, the carotenes and xanthophylls that color squash, carrots, and corn, and that give a leaf its yellow coloration when it loses chlorophyll. A plant

Some chlorophyll still survives on these just-turning Red Maple leaves.

grown in the dark can make no chlorophyll, but it can make carotenoids and therefore become yellow. A drought-afflicted leaf will lose chlorophyll, allowing the more stable carotenoids within to finally become visible. (In the leaves of beech and some oaks, tannins also may impart a yellow or brownish coloration.)

Finally, there is a third class of pigments found in tree leaves—the anthocyanins that produce the brilliant reds and purples we see in apples and grapes as well as in maples. But these are not found in chromoplasts. Instead, they are dissolved in the cell sap of the spongy tissues deep within the leaf blade. They form each fall by chemical reactions between accumulating sugars and organic compounds called anthocyanidins. Light is necessary for their development. Low temperatures above freezing and dry weather enhance their production. The more acid in the cell sap, the more dazzling the red; in sap that is alkaline, purple and blue predominate.

Substances other than pigments are also formed in

leaves. For example, there are resins that repel insects, and hormones that influence growth. Among the most important of the hormones are the auxins, which form in growing leaves. They seem to have numerous effects in the tree, from triggering the growth of new wood to causing ethylene gas to evolve, thus inducing flowering. Auxin production declines under drought conditions, so it is usually most highly concentrated in the spring, and then falls off during the summer as soil water gets used up. As summer progresses and the days shorten, the leaves get old, or senescent. This reduces their ability to make auxin and triggers the movement of nutrients out of the leaf, into storage in branches and trunk. Soon the balance of auxin and the growth-inhibiting hormone abscisin, becomes unfavorable, and a layer of corky cells develops where the leaf's stalk joins the twig. The leaf is now walled off from its tree; it cannot receive water from the sap stream, and cannot transfer the sugars that now thicken its cell sap.

Meanwhile, the chlorophyll balance is also changing, with destruction of the green substance outpacing manufacture. Then manufacture of chlorophyll ceases altogether, and the color green begins its retreat. Carotenes and xanthophylls are unmasked. Sugars trapped in the leaf sap react with anthocyanidins. The cool fires of autumn have been ignited.

How brightly these fires burn, and when, are important matters to leaf-peepers, especially those travelling great distances to view the spectacle. In general, the color change is predictable, but variable. Typically, fall colors in our region begin in late September and continue through October. The great wave of peak coloration starts in the north and at high elevations, and moves southward and downslope. The situation for a particular place during a specific year depends on several factors. It depends first of all on which tree species are present and what pigments they are harboring. Alders and black locusts, for example, have little pigmentation and hardly change color at all. Cottonwoods, birches, hickories, and some ashes are rich in carotenoids, but not in anthocyanins—so they paint the landscape gold and yellow. Red Maple, Sugar Maple, White Oak, Scarlet Oak and Sassafras are heavy with anthocyanins that produce deep wines and reds, and that can interact in some trees with carotenoids to produce the full spectrum of variation between red and yellow. Some trees surprise us. Quaking Aspen, for example, is usually thought of as bearing pure lemon-to-gold foliage; but in Michigan and elsewhere it occasionally produces anthocyanins that impart a distinctive orange or red coloration.

And it depends on the weather. Low temperatures help destroy chlorophyll and, if they stay above the freezing point, help create anthocyanin. Bright sunshine destroys chlorophyll and favors anthocyanin formation. Dry weather—even mild drought—speeds up anthocyanin synthesis. So the most brilliant fall foliage displays occur where the right combination of tree species combines the yellows of the carotenoids with the reds and purples of anthocyanin, and when dry, sunny days are followed by crisp, cool nights. These are the conditions that aid and abet the demise of green, the unmasking of yellow, and the formation of red. Because of its happy combination of the right tree species, and the frequent occurrence of the right weather conditions, our region leads the world in the beauty and fame of its fall foliage display.

But, as with other good things, this too has an end. The sealed-off leaves dry out, their chloroplasts and chromoplasts break down, their colors fade. The corky cells at the base of their stalks give way as leaves flex in the fall wind that plucks them loose and sends them to earth where they will await certain decay. The show is over.

SEEING THE SHOW

Fall is a special time in our region. Red and gold leaves, blue sky, and crisp temperatures make an unforgettable backdrop for the harvest of pumpkins, squash, apples, and grapes. It is festival time, with millions attending such events as the Giant Pumpkin Party, Cider Fest, Cranberry Harvest Fest, Apple Squeeze, Fabulous Fall Fishing Festival, and the Annual Falling Leaves Festival. In addition, there are the Peak Fall Color Weekend, Salute to Autumn, Fall Foliage Festival, Tomato Fest, Wine Country Circuit, Flaming Leaves Square Dance Festival, Saturday Evening Leaf Peeper Concerts, and Grape Stomping Festival. Antique cars, hot air balloons, sailplanes, horses, wine tasters, volunteer firemen, colonial militia, dog fanciers, jousting knights and chessmasters, wagon drovers and troubadours, ballerinas and polo players perform amid the splendors of autumn.

Deciding where the leaf peeping is best can be a frustrating task—like choosing a movie in a city of a thousand theaters. A general rule of thumb in any of the states and provinces of our region is to head for hilly rural areas. Hills and mountains create diverse habitats, ranging from wet valleys and marshes in the bottomlands to relatively dry slopes facing the south, shaded, frosty north-facing slopes, and windy peaks. This creates conditions for a wide variety of tree species and prolongs the period of peak color because of the downslope progress of coloration. Thus the popularity among fall travelers of Massachusetts' Berkshires, New York's Catskills and Adirondacks, the White Mountains of New Hampshire, the Green Mountains of Vermont, and Pennsylvania's Poconos. Lakes and ponds enhance the brilliance of fall colors, bringing many visitors to northern Minnesota and northern Wisconsin, Maine's Rangeley Lakes district, the Adirondacks, and southeastern Ontario. There are striking river roads that follow the St. Lawrence in Quebec, the Hudson in New York, the St. Croix between Wisconsin and Minnesota, and the beautiful Connecticut River reflecting landscapes of New Hampshire, Vermont, Massachusetts and Connecticut. National and provincial parks often create focal points, like Voya-

(opposite page)

Old woods roads offer the northeastern traveller intimate views of the hardwood forest.

9

geurs National Park in Minnesota, Isle Royale off Michigan's Upper Peninsula, the Papineau, Mont Tremblant, and Laurentides Parks of Quebec. Coastline drives add spice to tours around all the Great Lakes and on the Atlantic shores of New England, New Brunswick, and Nova Scotia. The various travel and tourism offices recommend areas they consider especially rewarding, but in the entire region from Minnesota to Nova Scotia, Quebec to Ohio, there is an almost infinite variety of wooded landscapes— ranging from the tranquility of New England villages to the wilderness of the Adirondack High Peaks. The most demanding traveler can find his or her personal Eden.

When is the best time to view fall colors? Color change is "predictable but variable." Late September to mid-October is usually reliably brilliant, but there is no substitute for local information. In recent years tourism officials have responded to the needs of travelers.

FALL COLOR HOTLINES

Many states and provinces in our region make available in the fall up-to-the-minute information on the progress of fall colors. Perhaps the most elaborate of these hotlines is that in use in New York. In that state the Division of Tourism receives hotline reports from a network of volunteer foliage watchers across the state. These are assembled into state-wide reports that are furnished to the media and are available to the public through a hotline telephone number. For example, on a recent mid-October weekend, peak color was reported in the Finger Lakes, Catskill, Thousand Islands-Seaway, and Adirondack regions, while the Niagara Frontier and Capital-Saratoga regions were approaching their peak. In the Chatauqua-Allegheny and Central Leatherstocking regions, fall colors were past their peak; but color was just getting started in the Hudson Valley and on Long Island. Similar reports are issued by most New England states, Ohio, and Ontario as well. Many daily newspapers, including *USA Today*, TV network morning programs, and weather channels display maps showing the progress of color change throughout the north. Local information is available from the following agencies.

Connecticut

Connecticut Travel Office
210 Washington Street
Hartford, CT 06106
1-800-243-1685; 203-566-3385

Delaware

Delaware Tourism Office
99 Kings Highway, Box 1401
Dover, DE 19903
302-736-4271

Illinois

Illinois Office of Tourism
State of Illinois Center
100 W. Randolf, Suite 3–400
Chicago, IL 60601
312-814-4732

Indiana

Indiana Tourism Development
    Division
Department of Commerce
One North Capitol, Suite 700
Indianapolis, IN 46204-2288
317-232-8860

Iowa

Iowa Department of Economic
    Development
Division of Tourism
200 East Grand Avenue
Des Moines, IA 50309
515-281-3100

Kentucky

Kentucky Department of
    Travel Development
2200 Capital Plaza Tower
Frankfort, KY 40601
502-564-4930

Maine

Maine Vacation Information
97 Winthrop Street
Halowell, ME 04347
207-289-2423

Maryland

Maryland Office of Tourism
    Development
Department of Economic &
    Community Development
217 East Redwood, 9th Floor
Baltimore, MD 21202
301-333-6611

Massachusetts

Massachusetts Division of
    Tourism
100 Cambridge Street
Boston, MA 02202
617-727-3232 (or 3201)

Michigan

Michigan Travel Bureau
P.O. Box 30226
Lansing, MI 48909
1-800-543-2937

Minnesota

Minnesota Office of Tourism
375 Jackson Street
250 Skyway Level
St. Paul, MN 55101
612-296-5029

Missouri

Missouri Division of Tourism
P.O. Box 1055
Jefferson City, MO 65102
314-751-3051

New Brunswick

New Brunswick Department of
    Tourism, Recreation, and
    Heritage
P.O. Box 12345
Fredericton, N.B. E3B 5C3
1-800-561-0123

New Hampshire

New Hampshire Office of
    Vacation and Travel
105 Loudon Road
P.O. Box 856
Concord, NH 03301
603-271-2666 (or 2343)

New York

New York Division of Tourism
One Commerce Plaza
Albany, NY 12245
1-800-CALL-NYS (for
    contiguous 48 States)
1-518-474-4116 (for other
    areas and Canada)

Nova Scotia

Nova Scotia Tourism
    Department
136 Commercial Street
Portland, ME
1-800-341-6096

Ohio

Ohio Office of Travel and
    Tourism
P.O. Box 1001
Columbus, OH 43266
1-800-BUCKEYE

Ontario

Ontario Travel
Eaton Centre
220 Yonge Street
Toronto, ON M5B 2H1
1-800-268-3735

Pennsylvania

Pennsylvania Bureau of Travel
    Development
416 Forum Building
Harrisburg, PA 17120
1-800-847-4872

Quebec

Tourism Quebec
770 Sherbrooke Street W.
14th Floor
Montreal, PQ H3A 1G1
514-873-2308

Rhode Island

Rhode Island Tourism
    Division
Greater Jackson Walkway
Providence, RI 02903
401-277-2601

Vermont

Vermont Travel Division
134 State Street
Montpelier, VT 05602
1-800-634-8984

Virginia

Director of Tourism
Virginia Division of Tourism
1021 E. Cary Street
Richmond, VA 23219
804-786-2051

West Virginia

West Virginia Division of
    Commerce
2101 Washington Street, East
Charleston, WV 25305
304-348-2200 or 2286

Wisconsin

Wisconsin Division of Tourism
123 W. Washington Avenue
P.O. Box 7920
Madison, WI 53707
608-266-2147

CHALLENGES FOR THE SERIOUS LEAF-PEEPER

In this chapter the coloration of leaves has been explained in terms of natural pigments and how they react to a changing environment. Other facts of leaf and bud life history are also discussed. The science-minded reader who really takes his or her leaves seriously, however, does not have to accept, without word, whatever the author has written. One can learn about leaves—as one can learn about almost anything—by one's self. In this spirit, we present a list of small experiments that can be performed with a minimum of equipment, and that will allow you to savor the experience of discovering for yourself what makes leaves tick.

1. Prove to yourself that winter buds really do contain leaves, or even flowers.

Late in the winter, or in early spring (February to March) clip some small branches from some leafless trees. Bring them indoors, and quickly put the cut ends in a vase of water. Within a few days the buds will burst and embryonic leaves will rapidly unfurl. Branches taken from high in the tree will be likely to bloom, as well as to leaf out. Some of the trees that can be "forced" most spectacularly are the poplars and aspens, horsechestnuts, and cherries.

2. Remove the chlorophyll and carotene from a summer leaf, and see whether any coloration remains.

Allow a green leaf to soak for one minute in boiling water; then place it in a tumbler of ethyl alcohol. Set the tumbler in a pan of water, to be kept warm for an hour or two. When the leaf is removed, it will be nearly colorless, and the alcohol will have become a green solution. The solution contains both chlorophyll and carotene pigments.

3. Remove the anthocyanin from red leaves, and show that it is sensitive to acidity.

Chop up half a cup of red leaves (for example: red maple, staghorn sumac, flowering dogwood) in a food processor, and place in a Pyrex® beaker. Cover with water, and heat almost to a boil. Keep it stirred. The red solution contains anthocyanin pigment. To a portion of the solution, add acetic acid (vinegar) drop by drop. Observe the color change. To your other portion of the solution, drop in small amounts of baking soda, which is alkaline. Observe the color change.

4. **Demonstrate that red pigment (anthocyanin) needs light for its normal development, but yellow pigment (carotene) does not.**

During the summer, cover part of a red maple leaf (or other anthocyanin-bearing species) with a double-thickness of masking tape. After the exposed part of the leaf has turned red in the fall, remove the tape. If the exposed area is yellow, anthocyanin has not formed beneath the shaded portion of the leaf.

5. **Determine whether the leaves of a tree consistently turn the same color year after year.**

Make color photos of several trees over a period of several years, making sure you catch them at their peak of color intensity. Be consistent about taking each tree's picture from the same point, at the same hour, and in full sunlight. Compare the photos over a period of three or more years.

6. **Measure the effect of its leaves on the growth of a shoot.**

Select ten buds of similar size on branch-tips of the same tree. When the young leaves emerge from these buds, pluck all of them from five of the shoots, leaving the other five as undisturbed "controls." After a month or six weeks, compare the lengths of the "plucked" shoots with those of the "control" shoots. A strongly deleterious plucking effect is most likely to be the result of growth hormone deprivation.

7. **Observe the continuing impact of leaf-eating insects through the season.**

Trace the outlines of some simply-shaped leaves (elm, birch, cherry, poplar) on squared paper ("cross-section" paper) soon after they reach full size. By counting the squares within the outline, compute each leaf's area. Compute also the area of holes or leaf tissue damaged by insect feeding, and determine the average proportion damaged. Do this about twice a month until leaf-fall. Show the seasonal trend of feeding damage on a graph.

Few leaves survive the summer without incurring some damage from leaf-eating insects.

trees of light

BEING A DESCRIPTION OF THE MAJOR
TREE SPECIES CONTRIBUTING TO THE
GREAT FALL SPECTACLE IN OUR REGION

Sugar Maple
(Acer saccharum)

"Much of the splendor of the northern forest in early autumn is due to the abundance of the Sugar Maple, which is then unsurpassed in brilliancy of color by any upland tree.... On some trees a part of the leaves turn scarlet and a part orange or yellow; on others all the leaves assume shades of bright clear yellow, and on others a few leaves become red or yellow on different parts long before the remainder lose their dark green summer color."

With these words, Charles Sprague Sargent (*The Silva of North America*, 1890) explained the central importance of the Sugar Maple to fall-foliage watchers throughout our region. The "Rock Maple," as it is sometimes called—thanks to its hard, heavy wood—grows on a variety of sterile and rich soils, in company with many of our area's major trees: Beech, Yellow and Paper Birches, Red and White Spruces, Basswood, Black Cherry, White Pine, White Ash, Oaks, and Hemlock. It can become established in the deep shade of thick woods, or on open slopes and bottomlands where it spreads a broad, rounded crown descending almost to the ground. Forest-grown specimens can exceed 130 feet in height, with straight column-like trunks clothed in deeply-furrowed gray bark, and may live for 400 years. Sugar Maple is one of the most useful trees in the North American forest, and its relationship with humankind has been long and productive. Its wood ("hard maple") makes the very finest of firewoods, yielding long-lasting glowing coals and high-quality charcoal. It is veneered for furniture, cabinet work, and musical instruments—except for their spruce soundboards, concert harps are sometimes made almost entirely of maple. It is turned for woodenware, bowling pins, shuttles, spools, and bobbins. It is walked on in the form of bowling alley floors, and danced upon in dance halls. It is a fine ornamental tree, and is being planted increasingly along streets as a replacement for elms killed by Dutch elm disease.

(opposite page)

Sugar made from sap of the Sugar Maple was an 18th-century staple.

(overleaf)

The fallen leaves of Silver Maple liven a dark forest pool in the upper midwest.

The Red-tailed Hawk is a common raptor throughout the range of the Sugar Maple.

But its greatest glory is its sap, for as Sebastien Rasles wrote, in his *Lettres édifantes et curieuses* (1724):

"There is no lack of sugar in these forests. In the spring the maple trees contain a fluid resembling that which the canes of the island contain. The (Indian) women busy themselves in receiving it into vessels of bark, when it trickles from these trees; they boil it, and obtain from it a fairly good sugar."

That "fairly good sugar" still flavors the syrup that millions of North Americans pour on their pancakes and ice cream, and forms the basis of a thriving maple products industry. Vermont leads the states by producing half a million gallons annually, New York is second with about 350,000 gallons, and Wisconsin third with about 125,000 gallons of the mellow liquid. Large quantities are produced also in Ontario, Quebec, and New Hampshire. The "sugarbush" is a far more automated place than it was in pioneer—and pre-settlement—days, with networks of plastic hoses having largely, but not entirely, replaced bark kettles and wood or tin buckets, but the rhythm of the sap-rise and the steamy scent of the sugarhouse are what they

(opposite page)

Seedlings of the shade-tolerant Sugar Maple often carpet the forest floor.

The leaves of some Sugar Maples turn a bright, clear yellow.

(opposite page)

Sugar Maple produces highly-valued wood products throughout our region.

were in times past. Maple sugar has had its place in history. Thoreau was a sugarer. John James Audubon feared that the "cuts and perforations made in their trunks" would injure the trees' health, and he urged farmers "to look to the preservation of their sugar-maples" (*A Maple Sugar Camp*, about 1833). To John Burroughs "a sap-run is the sweet good-by of winter. It is the fruit of the equal marriage of the sun and frost (*Signs and Seasons*, 1886)."

Sugar Maple even figured in the political philosophy of late eighteenth and early nineteenth century America. Sugar made from the boiling down of maple syrup was considered the product of free men, while cane sugar then becoming available from plantations in the West Indies was the product of the "toil, pain, and misery" of wretched slaves. Farmers' almanacs advocated the culturing of a maple sugar orchard as a patriotic task. In 1791, Dr. Benjamin

22

Rush of Philadelphia wrote Thomas Jefferson that when medical treatment required the use of sugar for a patient who refused to "benefit even indirectly from the labor of slaves," . . . "the innocent Maple Sugar will always be preferred. . . ." Rush praised Jefferson, who was reputed to have used only maple sugar, and to have established a sugarbush on his Virginia estate.

Sugar makers in Quebec, Ohio, and New York became alarmed, in the 1980s, over the reduced syrup production, or even the death, of many of their sugarbush trees. Acid rain and snow have been considered likely causes, especially on soils where their chemical activity cause toxic aluminum to become more freely available to tree roots. But, as sugar maker Willard Ives of Rensselaer County, New York points out, tent caterpillars and pear thrips have also been weakening many trees, and reducing their syrup yields. Cornell University extension forester David Taber adds that simultaneously with increased acid emissions in our region, trees have also been stressed by drought—and many sugarbush trees are approaching old age after a lifetime of receiving tapping injuries. So the decline of our Sugar Maples probably has deep and complex roots. Should the decline continue for long, all admirers of the Sugar Maple and its produce will rise with the late J. P. Brissot de Warville (*Nouveau voyage dans les Etats-Unis*, 1791) in his fervent wish that:

". . . there were formed from north to south a holy coalition to accumulate the produce of that divine tree, if, above all it were looked upon as an impiety to destroy so useful a tree. . . ."

Over much of the range of Sugar Maple grows also the Black Maple, a very similar species that had long been regarded as just a form of Sugar Maple with minor differences in its botanical characteristics. It is usually found in moist bottomlands and is reported to produce a syrup even better than that of Sugar Maple, with which it hybridizes, producing a confusing array of types.

Red Maple
(Acer rubrum)

Red Maple is perhaps the most common tree of our region, being at home almost everywhere from Newfoundland to Minnesota, Quebec to southern Florida. It is easily identified as a maple by its lobed leaves set in opposite pairs on the branchlet, and the fruit of paired samaras that quickly ripen in May or June. But its hallmark is the color red. In winter the buds and lustrous shoots are red. In April or May, the red maple flowers before most other trees, producing masses of bright scarlet blooms. The fruits are scarlet, the heavy wood is tinged with red—but most of all, the leaves, which may turn color as early as late August in dry years, produce a blazing scarlet that enlivens the many forests where this beautiful tree dwells.

(overleaf)

Red Maples are frequently intermixed with Sugar Maples.

Consider, as evidence, an experience of Henry David Thoreau, as recounted in *The Maine Woods*:

"We had not gone far before I was startled by seeing what I thought was an Indian encampment, covered with a red flag, on the bank, and exclaimed 'camp'! to my comrades. I was slow to discover that it was a red maple changed by the frost."

Red Maple is a lowland tree, and it is an upland tree. It grows in dark timbered swamps with Balsam Fir, and White and Black Spruces, where its early color change illuminates its more somber associates. It grows in dense hardwood forests with Beech, Yellow Birch, Sugar Maple, Basswood, and Hemlock. It aggressively invades open ground, and it lives in the shade of old forests. Its seeds germinate when they fall to the ground in late spring. Seedlings can grow rapidly, producing a handsome sapling with smooth grey bark over limbs carrying bright green leaves. Trees to 120 feet tall, 4½ feet thick, and 150 years old have been recorded but today only much smaller and younger ones can be found. Trees killed by fire, or removed by loggers, can put up vigorous sprouts from the stump, and vast areas of our forests are populated by Red Maple sprout clumps.

(opposite page)

A brilliant spray of foliage from a streamside Red Maple shoots the rapids of a northern river.

Red Maple and Quaking Aspen are aggressive invaders of forest openings.

ities, have allowed it to persist and even spread since our region was settled.

Red Maple is a preferred browse species of the white-tailed deer, and its seeds are eaten by rodents and grosbeaks. Its wood, which is not very strong or hard, places it in the group of the "soft maples," and is used for making boxes, furniture, and woodenware. Its syrup is less sweet and flavorful than that of the sugar maple, but is sometimes mixed with it in the kettle; and its incomparably scarlet fall foliage has made it popular in ornamental landscape plantings.

(opposite top)

This female American Redstart is one of the common warblers found nesting in the rich northern forests where Red Maples grow.

(opposite page)

The fruits of Sugar Maple, like those of all maples, consist of paired samaras, each containing one seed.

Silver Maple

Unkempt and brittle-branched, the Silver Maple is a popular ornamental nevertheless.

Silver Maple
(Acer saccharinum)

Silver maple gets no respect—affection, yes—but no respect. A prominent landscape architect accuses it of having "severe landscape handicaps." It grows too fast and looks unkempt. Its wood is brittle. The branches break too easily in the wind and under loads of ice and snow, littering the ground beneath it. Its roots are mischievous, lifting and cracking pavement, clogging drains and pipes.

And there is more. The wood is too wet, therefore susceptible to decay. The twigs emit a disagreeable odor when bruised. The flowers sometimes emerge so early in the spring they are destroyed by frost; and the sap, which—according to André Michaux—produces syrup the equal of that of the Sugar Maple, is too insufficient even to justify tapping. And, adding insult to injury, Wisconsin beavers avoid Silver Maple when there is something else to eat.

But despite the catalog of its faults and weaknesses, Silver Maple has plenty of admirers. They have planted Silver Maples by the million, in the "tax relief plantations" of Kansas and Nebraska during the 1860s and 70s, along their streets, outside their houses, and in their public parks. They have made it one of our most popular ornamental trees, whether it deserves that distinction or not. They enjoy watching the sharp-cut, silver-bottomed leaves turn clear yellow in the fall, and the delicate haze of pinkish-brown or greenish flowers appearing in the tree crowns in March or April, when other trees are still in winter's grip.Among Silver Maple's admirers was no less a figure than Charles Sprague Sargent, that sober collector of tree-facts, who unburdened himself a hundred years ago:

". . . (Silver Maple) forms a wide-spreading head, beautiful in the play of light and shade through the deeply divided leaves dancing with the slightest breath of wind on their slender stems and displaying the silvery whiteness of their lower surface."

Silver Maple is a tree of moist places, as attested to by some of its other names—Swamp Maple, River Maple,

(overleaf)

Leaves of Red Maple in the fall—the ultimate anthocyanin producers.

35

Maple buds and seeds—especially the large ones of Silver Maple—are among the preferred food of the Evening Grosbeak.

The deeply-incised leaf of Silver Maple distinguishes it from the other maples of our region.

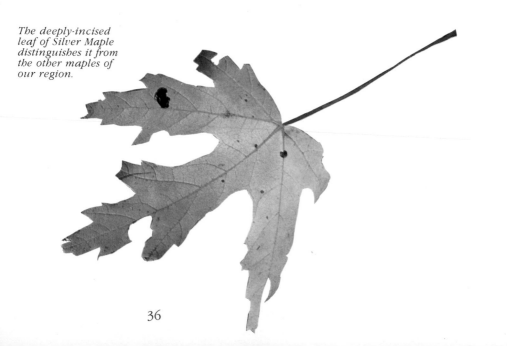

Creek Maple. It is found from Newfoundland to Florida, and west to the prairie borders of Nebraska, Kansas, and Oklahoma. In a typical Wisconsin habitat, the Tiffany Bottoms of the Chippewa River, it grows with American Elm, Red Ash, Swamp White Oak, River Birch, Hackberry, Basswood, Cottonwood, Sycamore, Bitternut Hickory, and Black Willow. Its early-flowering habit is, incidentally, not as suicidal as it appears: in most years the large, chestnut-brown seeds mature in April or May, fall immediately into freshly-deposited silt left by receding flood-waters, germinate, and produce vigorous seedlings that have several pairs of leaves by summer's end.

From New York and Pennsylvania west to Minnesota another soft-wooded maple grows on riverlands and swamp borders: the Boxelder. It is the only one of our maples with compound leaves, each of them bearing 3- to 5 long-pointed leaflets, and produces masses of dry samaras that hang in chain-like clusters through the winter.

Silver Maples carpet the surface of a sluggish stream with leaves no longer needed.

American Beech dominates many northern hardwood forests in our region.

American Beech
(Fagus grandifolia)

Wherever one travels in the vast hardwood forests from Nova Scotia to eastern Wisconsin, there grows the American Beech with its most constant companions, Sugar Maple and Yellow Birch. Beech is always recognizable by its clear, smooth, light gray trunks, its luminous leaves in their spring green, and the little triangular nuts paired in their prickly brown burs. American Beech is a medium-sized tree, but its trunks often appear massive, like the legs of mastodons; and it is said to have attained 161 feet in height. Because its thin bark dooms it to injury from ground fires and sun scald, and because the wood quickly decays on exposure, it does not live long; but the beech on which was carved the famous legend *D. Boone Cilled A Bar On Tree In Year 1760* was 365 years old when finally cut.

Beech has the habit of producing thickets of "root suckers," saplings arising from the roots, especially injured roots, and becoming trees in their own right. Its wood is hard and dense, useful for flooring, woodenware, furniture, and handles; and it is one of the finest fuel woods in our forest. The 3- to 5 inch-long toothed leaves are heavily browsed by white-tailed deer, and the bark was used by the Rapahannocks to make an infusion for treating poison ivy sores. But it is beechnuts that give this tree so much of its utility. The delicious nuts, or mast, that once were an item of commerce in the fall, provide man and animals with a food equal in energy value to bacon, but with twice the protein. The Iroquois pressed the oil from beechnuts, and used it for cooking. Early European settlers roasted the nuts to produce a coffee substitute. The nuts are eaten from the forest floor by mice, bears, raccoons, grouse, squirrels, and wild turkeys. But most important for the Beech, they are also eaten by blue jays. Simply put, jays plant Beeches. Recently, a flock of 75 blue jays were observed exploiting the beechnut crop in a Wisconsin woodlot in September. As the still-green beechnuts were maturing, jays removed them from their husks, accumulating an average of more than 7 nuts in their bills. They then

(overleaf)

Color change in leaves presages their death, and their ultimate return to the soil.

Blue Jays transport beechnuts and acorns up to 2½ miles, and cache them in the ground as stored food.

(opposite page)

Sugar Maples grow almost to the water's edge on the far bank of this northern river.

flew—as far as 2½ miles—to their former breeding territories, where the captured beechnuts were cached in the soil for future use. Damaged or diseased nuts were discarded at the source, so no energy would be wasted transporting them. These flights started about 6:30 in the morning, and continued until 6:30 at night, even in rain and high winds. Flights were often made along fencerows, where the jays could seek cover if they spotted a marauding hawk. During a 27-day period, they made over 13,000 flights and transported 100,000 nuts.

The buried beechnuts, hidden from rodents and other competitors in the soil of the jays' breeding territories, were destined to be used as food by the wintering jays and their future nestlings. But, when the beechnut crop is large, jays can be expected to hide more nuts than they and their young can consume, leaving a surplus that can germinate and produce new Beech trees. Eventually these jay-planted Beeches will feed new generations of jays who will plant new generations of Beeches which will . . .

Black Willow
(Salix nigra)

There are about ninety species of willows in North America, and about a third of them are tree-sized at least some of the time. There are dwarf willows growing in Arctic tundra, and tree willows in the Tropics. Although willows can be extremely difficult to identify, due mainly to variation within a species and hybridization between them, Black Willow is relatively easily recognized. It is the largest American willow, reaching heights of 60 feet or more, with massive, forked trunks clothed in thick, shaggy, brown, furrowed bark. Its long, tapered leaves are up to 8 inches in length, with fine-toothed edges. It is found in wet bottomlands, along streambanks, and on the margins of lakes and swamps. It has to be in full sunlight to thrive, but can withstand periodic flooding and partial burial in river-borne silt. All of the States and Provinces of our region play host to Black Willow, but in the Maritimes it is locally distributed. Trees that associate with it include American Elm, Red Ash, River Birch, Eastern Cottonwood, Boxelder, and Silver Maple. It grows fast, and dies young, seldom exceeding 80 years.

Black Willow—like others of its genus, and like its relatives the cottonwoods, aspens, and poplars—bears its flowers on catkins. Male and female catkins are on separate trees. The capsules arranged along the female catkins disperse light seeds in the wind that must land quickly on moist soil in order to germinate. But even if they do not, Black Willow can still spread, at least downstream. Its young shoots are brittle and designed to break off cleanly in the wind, allowing riverbank trees to virtually ship their branches downriver, where a chance landing on a sandbar will allow a branch to root and become established as a tree, doing business in a new location. The ease of rooting willow cuttings allows them to be used for stabilizing eroding banks. Stick them in wet soil and they will root in a matter of days.

Willows of all kinds were important to Indians of our region, who used the slender stems for basketry, and the

(opposite page)

A creekside Black Willow, its lance-like leaves stripped by an early snowstorm.

Willow foliage is a favorite food of the Moose.

(opposite page)

Black Willow is the largest member of its genus in North America.

bark to brew tea for curing lumbago, and weaving into a fabric. The wood made good bows, and the leaves were taken for fevers. The medical value of willow bark and leaves is due to the presence of the bitter, white, crystalline glucoside, salicin, from which is derived salicylic acid, which in turn yields aspirin. Thus, according to Ernest Thompson Seton, "a decoction of Willow bark and root is said to be the best known substitute for quinine." Many of our native species, like the Peachleaf, Pussy, Bebb's, and Shining Willows, are severely browsed by moose, where these large ungulates are still found; and, as a result, are maintained in a permanently bushy form, forming impenetrable thickets along mountain streams in the North Country.

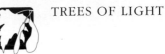

Paper Birch

(Betula papyrifera)

To Ernest Thompson Seton Paper Birch was "the white queen of the woods," the noblest of birches and the most bountiful provider of the northern forest. Its sap was boiled down to a sweet syrup said to have healing powers, and its inner bark, dried and pulverized, provided a flour in times of famine. The wood made fine frames for snowshoes and yielded hot coals in the fireplace. And of course there were the broad, tough sheets of chalk-white bark that provided shelter, containers, utensils, and transportation for the Indians and early settlers in our region. Those smooth, pliable, waterproof, bark sheets—Seton's "vegetable rawhide"—roofed uncounted settlers' shacks and forest wigwams. Craftsmen and women made the life of subsistence hunters easier by fashioning birchbark pots and pans, kettles and cups, spoons, pails, and boxes. Fine roots of spruce were used to sew up the seams of these implements, and these were waterproofed with pine or spruce pitch. Water could be brought to a rolling boil in a bark kettle by throwing in hot rocks from the fire pit. But the essential birchbark creation was the graceful canoe. Tough, buoyant, light in weight, repairable anywhere in the North Woods with common natural materials, the bark canoe was the skiff of Indian families and the galleon of war parties and *voyageur* fur brigades. Its graceful lines are still imitated in modern craft of aluminum or fiberglass, and rare artisans can still be found who build bark canoes in the traditional way.

The bark of Paper Birch, especially when split into thin layers, makes a tinder that is easily ignited wet or dry, throwing puffs of scented black smoke. Hollow cylinders of intact bark often mark the position of the fallen trunks they have outlasted. Stripped trunks do not regenerate new bark, but bear their scars throughout life, so bark-users should take their booty from dead trees or logs, or be satisfied with the small scrolls shed naturally.

Paper Birch is one of the widest-ranging trees of North America, spanning the continent from Newfoundland to

(opposite page)

Paper Birch ranges from Newfoundland to Alaska's Pacific coast.

The Timber Wolf inhabits the boreal forests of Paper Birch, Jack Pine, Balsam Fir, spruces and poplars.

(overleaf)

The gleaming white "vegetable rawhide" that covers Paper Birch trunks was made into many household products by woodland Indians.

(opposite page)

Pure stands of Paper Birch often become established on burned-over areas.

Alaska's Seward and Kenai Peninsulas. Over much of our region—in the Berkshires for example, and the Adirondacks—it grows scattered in mixed forests of pines, spruces, ash, fir, or maples. But further north, as in the Boundary Waters area of Minnesota and Ontario, it forms extensive pure stands on burned-over land. It is a pioneer on those burns, living a brief life in the sun only to be replaced by the spruces and other shade-tolerant trees that grow beneath it. Beavers eat its inner bark, deer and moose its twigs, and grouse its buds and flower catkins.

Paper Birch has rounded leaves and its bark is gleaming white. It should not be confused with the smaller Gray Birch, which has triangular leaves, and whose dingier bark is disfigured by triangular black scars below the junctions of branch and trunk. Gray Birch commonly forms stands of wispy, crooked stems on disused pastures and open roadside areas, especially in New England.

Yellow Birch
(Betula alleghaniensis)

After White Pine, Yellow Birch is probably the largest tree of the northern hardwood forests—the so-called beech-birch-maple community that covers so much of our area. In some of the wilder parts of the Adirondacks, Michigan's Upper Peninsula, and Quebec's *Parc de Laurentides*, it is still possible to encounter a ragged-crowned old Yellow Birch nearly a hundred feet high and four feet thick. It will probably be found in the company of Sugar Maple, Beech, Black Cherry, and Aspens, with Hemlocks, White Pines, Red Spruces and Balsam Firs within shouting distance. And it will most likely be growing on deep, rich, well-drained loams up to 2500 feet above sea level, where it will have been spreading wide its shallow roots for well over two centuries.

Trees like these are of considerable commercial value, as Yellow Birch's hard, close-grained wood makes fine furniture, kitchen cabinets, woodenware, butcher blocks, toys, toothpicks, and flooring. The white-toned wood takes stains well, and successfully masquerades as cherry or mahogany. When pulped, it makes high quality paper. And then there is wintergreen oil, that delightfully scented substance that makes the chewing of twigs on a hot summer day an exhilarating experience.

Both Yellow Birch and its close relation, the Sweet Birch, produce oil of wintergreen in their sap, leaves, bark, twigs, and roots. There was a time when young birches by the thousand were cut down, chopped up, and hauled to backwoods distilleries, where steam distillation extracted from them about a quart of oil per hundred saplings. Known chemically as methylsalicylate, a glucoside requiring enzymatic action for release of its ester, this aromatic oil has long been used for treating the pain of arthritis and rheumatism, and as a flavoring agent for candy and chewing gum. Today it is synthesized in laboratories.

Yellow Birch is immediately identifiable by its bark, which in all but very young and very old trees is smooth, lustrous, satiny, peels off in thin ribbons, and glows with

(overleaf)

Paper Birch and Sugar Maple produce hard, dense wood excellent in the campfire.

(opposite page)

A shaggy-barked Yellow Birch (center) shades a thicket of White Spruce saplings.

The fine twigs of Yellow Birch have bark rich in oil of wintergreen, and make pleasant chewing.

an indescribable color that has been variously described, nevertheless, as amber-yellow, pearly, silvery gray, and pale yellow gray. The highly inflammable bark curls, like that of Paper Birch, gives forth a fragrant, oily smoke, and assists in campfire-making in even the wettest weather. Yellow Birch is also distinguished by its prominent seed catkins, which persist through the winter, and its habit of growing on rotten logs which, when they decay into oblivion, leave the birch supported in mid-air on stilt-like roots.

"*Frequently*," writes Donald Culross Peattie,

(opposite page)

Yellow Birches crowd the rocky shore of a northern lake.

"*. . . when a Yellow Birch comes to the end of its lifespan, it stands a long time, though decay is going on swiftly under the bark. Such a tree is then nothing but a skin of bark stuffed with punkwood. Even this had its use, to the Indians; they collected and dried it, and carried it with them as tinder in which to start a fire by friction.*"

Black Cherry
(Prunus serotina)

This stately tree, found scattered in forests throughout our region, is the largest of the world's cherries—it is reported to have attained 129 feet in height and 7 feet in diameter. Trees so large are no longer found, because, with the exception of Black Walnut, Black Cherry produces the most valued wood found in our woodlands, and valuable trees are cut young.

The hard, heavy, bright reddish-brown wood produced on straight-boled forest-grown trees is known for its warm tone, which continues to mellow with years of exposure, and its absolute stability after it is seasoned. It is in demand for spirit levels, furniture, gunstocks, musical instruments, and even the bodies of fine large-format field cameras. The

(overleaf)

One of the Quaking Aspen clones flanking the Red Maple has begun to "yellow up"—the other is still green.

(opposite page)

Black Cherry trees usually grow from seeds excreted by fruit-eating birds during the fall migration.

Because of its highly-valued wood, Black Cherry has become hard to find in much of our region.

fame of Black Cherry cabinet veneers explains why this tree has also been called "Cabinet Cherry."

The trunk is wrapped in an aromatic, bitter bark that is shiny-red with raised horizontal ridges on young trees, that becomes roughened with small irregular plates on old ones. The bark is a source of prussic (hydrocyanic) acid, which is used in the pharmaceutical industry for making cough syrup and as an astringent. Another name for this species is "Rum Cherry," in honor of the pioneer Appalachian practice of steeping its edible but somewhat bitter fruits in rum or brandy to make "cherry bounce," a drink much favored.

The fruits, to half an inch in diameter, and red-black with purple flesh when ripe in September, attract numerous birds and mammals. Fall migrants like waxwings and thrushes pluck them from the tree tops, and digest the soft flesh. New cherry trees become established when the birds excrete the hard seeds into forest openings, or along fence lines, where they germinate and take root. Thus the typical scattered distribution of Black Cherry among Oaks and Ashes; Basswood, White Pine, Hemlock, and Elms; Black Walnuts and Maples.

Black Cherry's leaves are glossy deep-green above, with conspicuous tufts of orange hairs at the base of the midrib below. The flowers, which bloom after leaves unfold in May and June, are fragrant, white, and tiny, aggregated on spikes four to six inches long. Though they can live at least 200 years, most Black Cherries die sooner due to fires that sear the cambium beneath their thin bark, loss of foliage to defoliators like the tent caterpillar, or death of branches from infection by the disfiguring black knot disease.

There are also two shrubby species of cherry in our region. Chokecherry, which often becomes a small tree, has relatively wide leaves, and bears long spikes of very bitter, little, black fruits that pucker the mouth. Fire Cherry (or Pin Cherry) commonly grows up on burned-over areas, with Quaking Aspen and Gray Birch. It has narrow leaves and sour, red fruits.

Thickets of Fire Cherry frequently spring up on burned-over areas.

Red Foxes are among the many birds and mammals that feed on the bitter fruits of our wild cherries.

Quaking Aspen
(Populus tremuloides)

Quaking Aspen is found in every State and Province in our region—and well beyond. In fact, it grows as far north as Alaska's Brooks Range, south to Querétaro, Mexico, and east to Newfoundland—thus claiming the distinction of most widely distributed North American tree. It is instantly recognizable by its smooth, graceful trunks, ranging in color from creamy white to a yellowish green that approaches military olive drab. The round, silver dollar-sized leaves tremble in the faintest breeze on long, vertically flattened stalks, creating a rustling sound that serenades the ear, and a restless, quivering appearance like that of a tree viewed through heat-shimmering air. Thus the names "quaking" and "trembling" aspen.

"Quakies" are regarded as pioneers—trees that come in quickly and in large numbers on forest land recently logged or burned over. They do best in such open conditions, where they are never shaded, and where their rapid growth allows them to reach maturity in 15 to 20 years. Aspens are usually small trees that live less than a century, but hundred-footers have been found in the Lake States; and in the Rocky Mountains trees may live 200 years. When aspens are damaged by fire, logging, or heavy browsing by large animals, fast-growing stems emerge from their roots, creating thickets of "suckers." The suckers from the root system of a tree constitute a *clone*, a group of genetically-identical individuals that can persist for many hundreds of years by producing successive generations of new suckers. All members of a clone will be of the same sex, have bark of the same color, and have leaves that turn the same shade of color in the fall, on about the same date.

Unlike the bark of Paper Birch, which aspen superficially resembles, aspen bark cannot be peeled from the tree. The bark is easily scratched, exposing the inner green cortex tissue where photosynthesis occurs even in winter. Unfortunately, it is also easily scarred and can be defaced for decades by the carving of initials and valentines.

Aspens are useful trees. Their bark though bitter to us

(opposite page)

Quaking Aspen leaves that no longer tremble in the wind.

The inner bark of Quaking Aspen stems is a major food of the beaver.

(top)

The trembling of aspen leaves is owed to the flattened, flexible leaf stalks.

(overleaf)

Quaking Aspen's habit of forming clones results in large thickets of identical trees.

humans, is the preferred food of the beaver, and aspen stems often form the main structural elements of beaver dams. Ruffed grouse eat their winter buds, snowshoe hares dine on their twigs, moose and porcupines browse the foliage. Chippewa Indians drank the sweet inner-bark sap; and the Crees of the Hudson Bay region ate the inner bark. Thoreau was told by an Indian doctor that aspen inner bark could cure sore eyes. Both Indians and white settlers used bark preparations to treat fevers, as a laxative, to promote sweating, and as a cough remedy. An interesting inter-cultural tonic was prepared by combining the dried inner bark of aspen and dogwood with sarsaparilla root, until a quart jug was half-filled; then filling the rest of the jug with whiskey.

Aspen wood is soft, not durable, and relatively weak. It is widely used in paper manufacture, for excelsior, in boxes, and in crates.

Bigtooth Aspen is a very close relative of Quaking Aspen, and is similar to it in most respects. It grows throughout our region, but less commonly than Quaking Aspen, and can be distinguished from Quaking Aspen by its longer leaves with coarsely-toothed margins.

Aspens superficially resemble Paper Birch, but aspen bark does not naturally peel.

Balsam Poplar
(Populus balsamifera)

Throughout the northern part of our region, and in a broad subarctic band extending an incredible 113 degrees of longitude from eastern Newfoundland to the western peninsulas of Alaska, riverbanks and wet bottomlands are graced by a large poplar whose narrow crown is formed by a few rugged, ascending limbs. This is the *"Tacamahac"* of the Indians, the settlers' "Balm-of-Gilead," whose long, sticky buds yielded an aromatic resin or balsam— "very odorous, reminiscent of an admixture of sandalwood and onions," according to F. Schuyler Mathews— widely used for medicinal purposes. Buds boiled in bear grease, for example, made a dressing for wounds and eczema. Or, rubbed in the nostrils, a cure for bronchitis and congestion. Even heart trouble and miscellaneous pains and sprains could be treated with *tacamahac*, according to the Chippewas. The fragrant bud resin, amber in color, coats the surfaces of young leaves unfolding in the spring, acting as an insecticide against the larvae of defoliating insects. When the leaves mature, they are oval

(opposite page)

Balsam Poplar—the "Tacamahac"—is the most northerly of our poplars.

This Belted Kingfisher finds its prey in the same waters that nurture Balsam Poplar and the Eastern Cottonwood.

Balsam Poplar

Eastern Cottonwood is mainly distributed to the south of our region, but is commonly planted as a street tree.

or heart-shaped, up to six inches long, dark green above, light green with rusty, resinous blotches beneath, and edged with fine teeth. The twigs are shiny, smooth, and reddish-brown; and before opening, the buds may be an inch in length, shiny, sticky, and sharp-pointed at the tip. Like most other poplars and cottonwoods, Balsam Poplars are often short-lived, but some may attain 200 years. The perishable seeds that are carried by the wind from little capsules, arranged beadlike on drooping catkins, must find moist soil quickly in order to germinate. But Balsam Poplar can also reproduce itself by putting up suckers, or sprouts, from its roots, and many a small poplar grove is a clone formed in this way. Among Balsam Poplar's neighbors on the rich, moist soil of its preferred riverbank habitats are Willows, Alders, Paper Birch, Balsam Fir, and White and Black Spruces.

Besides its medicinal uses, this poplar has furnished pulp for magazine paper, lumber, excelsior, fuel, and—on Canadian shores of the Great Lakes—thick chunks of bark that served as fish net floats. It has also been planted on the plains of Manitoba and Saskatchewan as a shelterbelt tree. Balsam Poplar is easily propagated from stem cuttings: stick a foot-long spring shoot in moist soil, and it will root within days.

The Eastern Cottonwood, a massive and fast-growing riverbank dweller whose range is mostly to the south, is closely enough related to balsam poplar to hybridize with it freely. Its large broad-based ("deltoid") leaves, with their coarsely toothed margins, are not easily confused with Balsam Poplar's daintier ones, but the hybrid has leaves of intermediate width and can cause confusion for the amateur botanist.

Black Walnut

(*Juglans nigra*)

Pound for pound, inch for inch, Black Walnut is the most valuable tree in North American forests. Its deep-purplish-brown heartwood has long been in great demand by cabinetmakers, furniture manufacturers, gunstock carvers, and woodworkers. Much of it is veneered into thin sheets peeled off the log by a sharp blade. It was not always so: this tree, now rare in our forests (and in our region found only in southern Minnesota, Michigan, and Wisconsin, east through Ohio and Pennsylvania, in New York and southern New England, and in Canada mainly along Lakes Erie and Ontario), was once heavily logged and used even for fence rails and railway ties. In 1899 almost 39 million board feet were harvested, and seven years later the cut was over 48 million feet. The species was decimated. Changing times have made walnut's hard, close-grained wood, once undervalued, a commodity so sought after that rare large specimens have been auctioned on the stump for up to $30,000. But wood is not the only fine produce of this tree. The nuts—comparable in food energy value to bacon, in

Black Walnut trees grown in the open produce large crops of tasty nuts.

*The yellowing leaflets
of Black Walnut will
fall individually, leav-
ing the long, bare leaf
stalks projecting from
the branches.*

protein to lean leg of lamb, and rich in potassium, iron, and phosphorus—are gathered wild and used in ice cream and cookies. Run-of-the-woods mature trees can produce 3,000 or so ripe nuts in October of a crop year, and one grand tree has been known to double that. The stone-hard corrugated shells that contain the sweet nut-meats are themselves enclosed in thick, fleshy, aromatic, green husks that form dangling spheres to 3 inches in diameter. These are a major attraction to gray squirrels and fox squirrels who harvest them, carry them 50 to 100 feet, and bury them singly in the soil as food caches. Neglected nuts often germinate, producing the seedlings that form the next Black Walnut generation. This arrangement, an example of a mutualistic relationship between a plant and an animal, is typical of those found among trees with large, heavy seeds.

Most forest-grown Black Walnut trees are found singly or in small groves. They cannot tolerate shade, and tend to dominate such neighbors as White Ash, Basswood, Beech, Sugar Maple, Oaks, and Hickories. Black Walnut has long been known to emit a toxic substance called *juglone* from its roots. This compound is antagonistic to the growth of nearby plants, and may assist Black Walnut by

76

helping to keep in check competing vegetation. Similar "allelopathic" effects have been discovered among numerous other plants.

Black Walnut trees have been reported to attain 150 feet in height with trunks up to 8 feet in diameter at breast height. Maximum age seems to be about 250 years, but given their great value, few trees are likely to be allowed to live so long.

A close relative of the Black Walnut is Butternut, or the White Walnut. Like Black Walnut, Butternut has large compound leaves, but they usually bear 15–23 leaflets instead of Black Walnut's 11–17 leaflets; and the husk of the Butternut is oblong in shape, with a pointed end, unlike Black Walnut's spherical husk. Butternut husks contain a water-soluble brown dye that early pioneers used on homespun cloth, and the immature fruits were pickled in spiced vinegar as a frontier delicacy. In recent years Butternut trees have been heavily infected by tree-killing *Sirococcus* cankers, caused by a fungus that has spread rapidly to almost all of Butternut's range. Whether the species can withstand this sudden new onslaught is as yet undetermined.

(left) Beneath these aromatic, fleshy husks lie the hard-shelled, nutritious walnuts. (right) The Gray Squirrel buries walnuts away from the parent tree. If forgotten nuts sprout, they will be out of their parent's shade.

White Oak
(Quercus alba)

White Oak is a stately forest tree common across most of our region, but just barely reaching far enough north to call southern Ontario and Quebec its home. It is found on relatively dry, sandy plains, rich uplands, and well-drained bottoms. Grown in the open, it spreads great limbs to form a dome-shaped canopy.

This species can be recognized in the fall by its 5- to 9-inch long leaves with their 7 to 9 rounded lobes, its light ashy-gray bark, and oblong acorns fitted into warty cups. The leaves make their spring debut as tender little rose-colored appendages, then become glossy-green on top and hairy whitish below, change into fall hues of wine-red, and finally turn light brown as they wither and fall.

White Oaks can be magnificent. The giants that greeted early colonists are almost all gone now, but some reached 150 feet in height with trunks eight feet through. Ages of 600 years were not uncommon.

This is a tree that has always enjoyed respect. Indians of the eastern woodlands ground the acorns into a flour which they baked into a nutritious bread. Pioneers in our region emulated their Indian neighbors, but also made extensive use of the hard, heavy, light-brown wood, considered the finest all-around wood of American forests. It made excellent cabin beams, lumber, shingles, posts, and fence-rails. On July 5, 1758, Lord Howe and General James Abercrombie attacked the French at Ticonderoga with a fleet of nine hundred 35-foot *bateaux* built of white oak. In the next war, such colonial ships as the frigate *Constitution* were fabricated of White Oak decking, knees, and keelsons. Today, White Oak is still in demand for parquet flooring, furniture, veneer, firewood, and—that unique product of such great importance to the distilling industry—whiskey barrels. To discriminating sippers of the corn, fine old bourbon not aged in White Oak barrels is unthinkable.

Forest animals also appreciate White Oak. Wood ducks are among the most voracious eaters of White Oak acorns,

(overleaf)

A miscellany of leaves from the northern hardwood forest.

(opposite page)

White Oak, the most famous and useful of American oaks, was called "Stave Oak" because of its use in whiskey barrels.

Ripe acorns are a favorite food of many forest animals, especially raccoons.

but these are also favored by ruffed grouse, purple grackles, brown thrashers, red-headed woodpeckers, black bears, and raccoons. Gray squirrels bury acorns for future use, but they must solve a problem posed by the acorns. White Oak acorns, unlike the seeds of many trees, are ready to sprout as soon as they come off the tree in the fall. But when acorns sprout, their nutrients are transferred into the new seedling, reducing the acorn's food value. Grey squirrels avert this by chewing off the pointed acorn tip that gives rise to the seedling root, preventing germination and keeping the acorn dormant, and therefore safe to bury as a future food source.

A close relative of White Oak that occurs in all States and Provinces of our region, except New Hampshire and Nova Scotia, is the Bur Oak. It can be distinguished from White Oak by the generally larger leaves, which have deep divisions (almost to the mid-rib) on the lower part of the leaf, and shallow ones on the upper leaf. Its acorns are very large—up to two inches in length—enclosed in deep, hairy cups ("burs"). In fall the leaves turn a dingy brown, or, at best, a dull golden yellow. The ability of this tree's thick bark to resist grass fires has allowed it to survive in the "oak openings" of southern Wisconsin, where it can be found scattered amid prairies.

The lobes of Red Oak leaves (left) are sharp and bristly, while those of White Oak are rounded.

Northern Red Oak
(Quercus rubra)

This tree is the most widespread of the northern oaks, and extends across every state and province in our region. But like some others of our forest trees, it is a relative newcomer, having moved in from the south during the past 13,000 years, following the retreat of the great ice sheet. That may have been a mistake, because Northern Red Oak is having difficulties in its new home.

In New York and New England it has been under attack for over a century by the gypsy moth, a European insect that was shortsightedly imported into Boston by an incurable optimist who planned to use the larvae as silkworms. His optimism was excessive—the moth has since spread south to Maryland and west to Michigan where its larvae feed voraciously on the leaves of oaks and numerous other species. Gypsy moth populations now appear to be establishing themselves on the West Coast and in the Rocky Mountains.

Another pest afflicting Northern Red Oak is the oak wilt, a fungus-caused disease that kills when fungal growth clogs the water-conducting sapwood by causing gummy blockages to form. The lack of water causes leaves to wilt, and results in quick death. The wilt can spread the old-fashioned way, when sap beetles that get covered with fungal spores while foraging on infected trees inadvertently transfer them to open wounds on uninfected trees. But oak wilt can also spread more stealthily, by the movement of spores through interconnected roots of neighboring trees. This is made possible by the large, open pores in the sapwood of Red Oaks and their close relatives—trees of the "red oak subgenus"—all of which are more at risk than are those of the "white oak subgenus," whose tightly constructed wood is less navigable to fungal spores. It is for the same anatomical reason that White Oak barrels hold liquids, but Red Oak barrels had best be filled with drop-forged nails or soda crackers. Oak wilt is a problem in the southern parts of our region, in forests and in landscape plantings of Red, Scarlet, and Pin Oaks.

(opposite page)

Northern Red Oak arrived in our region as the great glaciers of the Ice Age receded.

Black Bears are important consumers of red oak and black oak acorns, which are rich in carbohydrates.

Unlike trees of the white oak group, those of the red oak group have acorns that take two years, not one, to mature. The inch-long nuts of Northern Red Oak acorns fall from their flat cups (as Ernest Thompson Seton writes of this acorn, *"in fact it has no cup, it has a saucer"*) in the autumn, and become prey to mice, weevils, birds, and squirrels. The squirrels who cache them underground do *not* bite off, or "notch," the pointed acorn tips to prevent germination while in overwinter storage, as they do with White Oak, because they know that Red Oak acorns do not germinate until spring. At that time, surviving acorns put down a long tap-root, and grow more rapidly than most oaks for a potential lifetime of about three centuries. The wood is used in numerous interior applications, notably as flooring, cabinets, desks, chairs, and doors. In places as far away as France and Argentina Northern Red Oak is grown in forest plantations for the production of hardwood.

Trees of the red oak group are variable, they often look

(opposite page)

Northern Red Oak is a common inhabitant of sandy and rocky soils, as well as deeper loams and clays.

alike, and they are hard to tell apart. Worse yet, they often hybridize, causing much confusion in identification. Northern Red Oak can be distinguished from its close relative Black Oak by having 7–11 lobes on its leaf (instead of Black Oak's 5–7 lobes), and by its saucer-like acorn cup attached to an inch-long nut (vs. black oak's ⁵/₈-inch nut). Due to the difficulty of red-oak identification, it has escaped notice until recently that in extreme southwestern Ontario, and in the Niagara region, grows the Shumard Oak, a southern species here found about ninety miles north of its previously recognized range. It was long confused by its resemblance to the Northern Red Oaks, Pin Oaks, and Black Oaks growing in the vicinity. Certainty in oak identification often requires specialized knowledge.

Black Oak, perhaps the most common red oak-group species after Northern Red Oak, is absent from the Maritimes but otherwise broadly distributed in our region. It grows with other oaks and hickories, especially on poor sandy soils. Because of its short, crooked trunks and large limbs it has never been an important timber tree. Before aniline dyes were invented, however, its inner bark was the source of *quercitron*, a powerful and brilliant dye that, combined with various mordants, could produce hues of bright yellow to orange in fabrics ranging from fine silks to woolens. Thus the names Quercitron and *Chêne des teinturiers* (dyers' oak), have also been applied to the Black Oak.

(opposite page)

Leaves on diseased or broken branches often lose their green color prematurely.

(opposite page)

Acorns of Northern Red Oak need two years to mature.

White Ash
(Fraxinus americana)

Ashes have compound leaves made up of several leaflets attached in opposite pairs to a central stalk, with a single leaflet at the tip of the stalk. Most ash leaves have 7–9 leaflets. These leaves are themselves attached to the woody growth in opposite pairs, and the branches of ashes leave the stem also in opposite pairs. Among the trees of our region, only the maples and dogwoods share this trait of opposite leaves and branches, though it is also found among shrubs of the honeysuckle family. All ashes can be distinguished further by the clusters of dry fruits, shaped like the blades of canoe paddles, that hang on through the winter.

The most common of our ashes is the White Ash, found almost everywhere in our region but only in the southeastern part of Minnesota. It usually occurs on rich upland soils in woods of Sugar and Red Maples, Yellow Birch, Hemlock, Oaks, Hickories, Black Cherry and Beech.

It is the wood of White Ash that makes this tree notable, for it combines in an exceptional way toughness, hardness, relatively light weight, and the ability to be bent into strongly curved shapes after steaming. Toughness and resilience have made White Ash the wood of choice for baseball bats—a few are fashioned from hickory, but over a million are made annually from White Ash, which is lighter and just as tough. The best whitewater canoe paddles are of White Ash, as are the keels and thwarts of better canoes.

Steam-bent White Ash is the only respectable material for fine, handmade snowshoes designed to resist decades of flexing and bending in soft snow. Lacrosse racquets, hockey sticks, and shovel handles are among other specialized uses of this superior wood. The summer visitor to a woodland containing White Ash can also benefit from the ability of its crushed leaves to take the pain out of a bee sting.

Two other ashes can be found in our region. The Black Ash is a dweller of swamp-borders and streambanks. Some of its typical associates are Tamarack, Red Maple, Balsam

(opposite page)

White Ash is usually scattered in forests of numerous hardwood species.

91

(overleaf)

When crushed and applied to a bee-sting, White Ash leaves take away the pain.

Poplar, Spruces, and Arborvitae. Indians used its logs, which when pounded could be split into thin strips, for basket-weaving material, fashioning from them such utilitarian items as the famous Adirondack pack-basket. Black Ash can be distinguished from all other ashes by the lack of any stalk at the base of its leaflets—the leaflets are attached directly to the central stalk of the large compound leaf. The Green Ash, also called Red Ash, is widely distributed throughout our region and further south and west. It is usually found along riverbanks and around swamps, and can often be identified by the hairiness of its new branchlets. It is an important shade tree and is often planted in shelterbelts in the Midwest.

The Purple Finch, seen here feeding on fleshy fruits, also consumes large numbers of dry ash seeds.

Shagbark Hickory
(Carya ovata)

"It is a tree of many excellencies," said Ernest Thompson Seton of the Shagbark Hickory, the best known of the hickories found in our region. Most people who recognize this species distinguish it by the great strips of thin gray bark that partially peel off the trunk, hanging for years before falling. But this tree has other splendid qualities that have almost been forgotten in this age of plastics and other synthetic materials.

Wherever wood is appreciated, hickory is admired; and Shagbark is the best of the hickories. As a fuel, it is unsurpassed in the North American forest for its ability to produce heat even when green, and to form long-lasting, glowing coals. Hickory-smoked hams and bacon are a famous legacy of the American pioneer past. The tough, heavy, elastic wood is also unsurpassed for uses where

The husks of Shagbark Hickory split in fourths, exposing the large, delicious nuts.

95

impacts are incurred, as in handles for axes, picks, hammers, and sledges. In his *Report on the Trees and Shrubs Growing Naturally in the Forests of Massachusetts* (1878), George B. Emerson enumerated some of the many uses of hickory wood in the 1800s: screws; handles for pitchforks, chisels, augers, gimlets, and axes; mallets and beetle-heads; handspikes and sail-rings for sailing vessels; cogs for grist mills; springs for gigs, whiffletrees for stage-coaches, and shafts for wagons; hay-rake teeth, axletrees, and barn floors. More recently it has been important in chairs, skis, gymnastic bars, ladders, sucker rods and picker sticks, dowels and skewers. Even the ashes of hickory were prized, for the manufacture of soap.

But if its wood was admired, Shagbark Hickory's succulent nuts were savored above all others. Hickory nuts are oval to globose, thick-shelled, and enclosed within a thick yellowish husk, measuring about two inches in diameter. The husk splits cleanly into fourths, liberating the nut, and making it freely available to the variety of wildlife that feed upon it—grey squirrels, fox squirrels, flying squirrels, red squirrels, white-tailed deer, wild turkey, quail, and raccoons. Nuts buried by squirrels, and forgotten or not needed, often germinate and produce hickory seedlings. There are about a hundred nuts to the pound. Hickory nuts were greatly prized by Indians, and William Bartram (*Travels Through North and South Carolina, Georgia, East and West Florida*, 1792) observed among the Creeks family stockpiles exceeding a hundred bushels. They were eaten whole, or pureed as an ingredient of hominy and corn cakes. Hickory nuts were an important item in the American nut market until the cultivation of the pecan hickory made larger, thinner-shelled nuts widely available. Even the sap of Shagbark Hickory is reputed to have made an exceptionally tasty sugar.

The Shagbark Hickory grows throughout the southern part of our region, north into southern Maine, the St. Lawrence Valley and southwestern Quebec, in Ontario from the lower Ottawa River Valley to Lake Huron, and west to southeast Minnesota. Southward it ranges deep into Dixie. It has fragrant compound leaves bearing five leaflets, and is said to have attained a height of over 130 feet. One encounters it in mixed hardwood forests below 2000 feet

The loose, shaggy bark plates of Shagbark Hickory were used in pioneer days as the source of green and olive dyes for woolen fabrics.

elevation, especially with oaks.

Our region, especially the southern part of it, is also host to two hickory species that do not have exfoliating bark. These are the Pignut and Mockernut Hickories. The Shellbark Hickory does shed strips of bark, and is much like Shagbark Hickory, but is usually found on wet bottomlands. Hickories often hybridize, so certain identification of these species can be problematic.

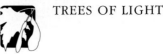

Basswood
(Tilia americana)

Within our region only Nova Scotia does not know Basswood. Otherwise it is one of the most common of our trees, found in forests of Sugar Maple, Yellow Birch, and Black Cherry; with Hemlocks and White and Red Oaks; and in low-lying woods where White Ash and American Elm luxuriantly grow. These are rich woods with deep, moist, black soils, and in them Basswoods can reach heights over 130 feet with diameters of 3 to 4 feet.

It is a handsome tree with large heart-shaped leaves, coarsely toothed on the margin; smooth gray or green bark becoming brown and ridged with age; and a broad, rounded crown. Basswood sprouts vigorously, and it is common to find a circle of young trunks surrounding the stump of an old one. But much of Basswood's distinction is lent by its flowers and fruits. Hear, for example, naturalist Donald Culross Peattie on the early summer blooming of the Basswood, or American Linden, as he preferred to call it:

(opposite page)

Basswood has been prized for products as varied as honey, cordage, and box-wood.

"When the shade begins to be heavy and the midges fill the woods, and when the western sky is a curtain of black nimbus slashed by the jagged scimitar of lightning, when the wood thrush seldom sings except after rain and instead the rain crow, our American cuckoo, stutters his weary, descending song—an odor steals upon the moist and heavy air, unbelievably sweet and penetrating."

The nectar of those sweet-scented flowers is highly attractive to honeybees, who swarm in the tree crowns to gather it, and make of it a strong-flavored honey of fine quality. The white-petaled flowers, which are a mere half-inch in length, are arranged in small groups attached to a central stem itself attached to a unique leaf-like bract, up to 5 inches long and narrowly oblong. When the flower ovaries mature to fruit, a group of hairy, grayish, pea-sized nutlets continues to dangle from the bract, sometimes re-

The heart-shaped leaves of Basswood are among the largest simple leaves in our forest.

(opposite page)

Paper Birch graces the shore of many a northern lake.

maining into the winter, until thrushes or jays pull them off. The wood of this tree is soft, light, white, and weak. It is excellent for carving and was used by the Iroquois of New York for their ceremonial false-face masks. It has been used for boxes and crates, yardsticks, window-sash, and pulp. Quantities of it were sliced into excelsior, but plastic foams have largely replaced that product. The bark had several uses in earlier centuries, including the manufacture of rope and cord from the inner-bark fibers. Indians stripped it from the tree in springtime, wrapped it around a rock to keep it submerged in a creek for a month, then twisted it to form soft, tough lengths that, it is said, do not kink when dry. Basswood leaves are a favorite summer food of porcupines.

American Elm
(*Ulmus americana*)

Half a century ago this greatly admired elm seemed secure in its position as the most-planted street tree throughout our region. Countless village and city streets boasted avenues lined with towering White Elms, as they are often called; while public parks and college campuses between the Mississippi and the Atlantic almost invariably were similarly adorned. But no longer. Today Minneapolis' elms are gone—replaced by Hackberry trees. The elms of Camden, Maine, have been hauled away and burned; and Sugar Maples put in their places. Syracuse, New York, has cut down its dead or threatened elms, and to be on the safe side, sacrificed also some cottonwoods and Silver Maples.

Farmsteads and junctions from Bellows Falls, Vermont, to Sturgeon Falls, Ontario, must now be shaded by oaks or pines, for nearly all of the great elms are gone. Their fate, sealed by Dutch elm disease, is one of the tragic stories of our forest, and one whose final chapter is yet unwritten.

American Elm is a distinctive tree. At close range, it can quickly be recognized by its leaf—up to 6 inches long, with a doubly toothed margin, long-pointed tip, and asymmetrical base. In the spring, the leaves are preceded by masses of reddish brown flowers borne in loose, pendent clusters. These soon mature, becoming flattened oval samaras—dry fruits—each bearing one seed in its center. The samaras tumble from the treetops and are dispersed in the wind or on the surface of running water. From a distance American Elm displays its unique champagne-glass shape, created by the graceful arching of the several divisions of its trunk. This form, which has been compared to that of a vase or a feather duster, allows open-grown elms in fields and pastures to be identified from a mile or more. Great spreading-crowned elms as much as thirteen feet in diameter and 160 feet in height have gained fame for the treaties that were signed in their dappled shade or for their size alone, which made them landmarks. The wood of this species is tough, hard, and difficult to split because of its

(opposite page)

American Elm was once the shade tree of choice in the towns and pastures of our region.

interlocking grain. When it was available it was used for barrel staves and hoops, wagon-wheel hubs and spokes, bentwood furniture, and fruit-box veneer. It has grayish-white sapwood, a light brown heart, distinct growth rings, and no taste or odor.

American Elm, which grows throughout every State and Province in our region, is typically a tree of wet bottoms and flats where water stands in the spring or fall. It grows in mixture with Red and Silver Maple, Eastern Cottonwood, Basswood, and Black Ash. Many solitary trees have grown to great size in meadows, where they were left standing to shade livestock.

Dutch elm disease is caused by the fungus *Ceratocystis ulmi*, which changed the outlook for American Elm when it arrived from Europe before 1930 on imported elm logs. The spores of the fungus are carried about by two species of elm bark beetle, one of them native, the other European. Adult beetles—built like bulldozers a tenth to an eighth-of-an-inch long—bore into the inner bark and outer sapwood of healthy elms, and, while feeding, accidentally deposit in their galleries spores that adhered to them while feeding earlier in a diseased tree. Spores can now germinate and produce invading strands of tissue—hyphae—that proliferate within the water-conducting sapwood cells, killing them, turning them deep brown in color, and destroying their ability to supply water to the thirsty young leaves above. Spores can also ride up the sap stream, as they can fit through the perforations between conducting cells. Or they can pass across natural root grafts into the sapwood of a neighboring tree. Within a month the leaves of some branches wilt and turn brown. By summer's end, a newly infected tree may be dead. Individual elms of high value can be protected from the beetles by spraying, or by removing dead or dying branches, or even chunks of elm firewood that attract the beetles as breeding places. Protection from the fungus by injecting trees with an antibiotic has not been successful. A chemical toxic to the beetles can be injected every few years into trees of high value, but is too expensive to be used on elms scattered in natural forest. So it appears we will have to do without great old elms in our pastures, our woods, and our towns. Dutch elm disease may not have the ability to make our

elms extinct, but it will probably prevent them from ever again becoming great or old.

Two other related species, the Slippery Elm and the Rock Elm, occur in parts of our region. Neither has the characteristic form of the American Elm, nor are they as common.

Today, groups of trees like these are becoming rare, as elms are killed by the Dutch elm disease.

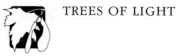
Tamarack
(Larix laricina)

The bogs and timbered swamps of our region are frequently graced by the presence of Tamarack, the only northeastern cone-bearing tree that sheds its needles in the fall and stands leafless over the winter. During September and October the bright green needles turn suddenly "smoky gold," as forester-naturalist Aldo Leopold once put it. They drift to earth and are replaced by new spring growth developing mainly in needle clusters on short, peg-like, woody shoots. Thus they add subdued brilliance to usually-somber woods inhabited by Balsam Fir, Northern White-Cedar, Black and White Spruces, and the brighter Alders, Bog Birch, and Black Ash. Though absent from most of Ohio and southern Pennsylvania, tamarack is widely distributed throughout the rest of our region in cold, wet places whose climates mimic those of the far northern woods, stretching from Newfoundland to Alaska, where most tamaracks grow. Indeed, Tamarack is found

(opposite page)

Tamarack is the only coniferous tree of our region that turns yellow and drops its needles in the fall.

These peg-like short shoots from which the needles have fallen, and the tiny seed cones, are characteristic of Tamarack.

well north of the Arctic Circle, and can withstand the range of temperatures from −78 to 100°F.

Tamarack is a small- to medium-sized tree with a pyramidal crown of slender, feathery, ascending branches. It produces small cones less than an inch long, made up of about 20 stiff scales. The seeds borne in these cones are about half an inch in length, most of which is in the delicate wing that catches the wind when the seeds tumble out of opened cones in the fall and early winter. Weighing only about a sixteen-thousandth of an ounce, a Tamarack seed can be carried long distances from its mother tree. Those not eaten by small rodents germinate, especially if they fall on bare soil, and grow rapidly unless shaded by other plants.

Numerous fungal diseases may kill Tamaracks that survive their youth, but the most serious enemies of these conifers are the larch casebearer (a native of Europe and Asia that has spread rapidly in American forests of Tamarack and Western Larch) and the larch sawfly. The caterpillars of these pests eat the new spring needles in great number, often killing the tree in the first year of infestation.

(opposite page)

The pyramidal shape of young Tamaracks results in part from its fast-growing leading shoot.

Shallow-rooted Tamarack may be thrown over by strong winds, or the roots cooked by forest fires burning in ground litter. Porcupines kill trees by chewing off bark to bare wood; and beavers by flooding Tamarack swamps with their dam building.

Tamarack wood is very strong, heavy and hard, and resists rot in contact with the ground. As early as the seventeenth century, chronicler John Josselyn complained that while foundations made of Tamarack "will never rot . . . you may almost drive a nail into a bar of Iron as easily as into that." Josselyn also recommended treating wounds with Tamarack resin, and had good luck using a mixture of crushed Tamarack needles and hog fat. Today Tamarack logs yield a gum, arabinogalactan, used in making baking soda, and the wood is used for lumber, poles, plywood, and paper pulp.

(overleaf)

Tamaracks show where the bogs are, in the northern forests of our region.

The scent of crushed Sassafras is the most unforgettable aroma of the eastern forest.

Sassafras
(Sassafras albidum)

Sassafras is a medium-sized tree found in hardwood forests in the southern part of our region, and southward. Its smooth-margined leaves, which can be unlobed, mitten-shaped, or 3-lobed, and the spicy odor of its foliage and twigs, are unique. It bears dark blue cherry-like fruits that dangle from red stalks.

American Mountain-Ash
(Sorbus americana)

(opposite page)

The tiny-apple-like fruits of American Mountain-ash feed Ruffed Grouse and Cedar Waxwings in the fall and winter.

Common in forests of our region, this small tree bears compound leaves of 13 to 17 long, pointed leaflets, and masses of bright red little fruits that look like miniature crabapples. The related European mountain-ash bears red-orange fruits, and is a popular shade tree.

Red-Osier Dogwood grows along stream-banks throughout our region.

Hawthorns make excellent ornamental plantings and "living fences."

Red-Osier Dogwood
(Cornus stolonifera)

This red-stemmed shrub, also called "Kinnikinnik," grows on streambanks from coast to coast. Its tree-sized cousin, Flowering Dogwood, is a forest dweller with showy white flowers in spring and brilliant red foliage in the fall.

Red Mulberry is found on moist soils in our more southerly hardwood forests.

Red Mulberry
(Morus rubra)

This medium-sized tree, found in the southern parts of our region, bears delicious inch-long fruits that look like blackberries. Like Sassafras, its leaves may be unlobed or lobed, but they are toothed on the margin while those of Sassafras are not.

Hawthorn
(Crataegus spp.*)*

There are many species of Hawthorn (or Thornapple) in our region, usually found invading pastures or along creeks. They bear strong thorns, and small, apple-like red or orange fruits that are favorites of foxes and many bird species.

Hackberry is also called "Sugarberry" for the small red to purple fruits eaten by many birds and mammals.

Hackberry
(Celtis occidentalis)

Found mostly in the western part of our region, this is a medium-sized tree often found growing on limestone. It is a close relative of the elms, and has similar wood. It has characteristic little warty growths on its bark and bears small cherry-like fruits with a netlike pattern on the surface.

Black Tupelo
(Nyssa sylvatica)

(opposite page)

Black Tupelo, or "Blackgum" is most at home in the bottomlands of the Atlantic coastal plain.

If not for its alternately-arranged leaves and blue fruits, often clustered in 2s or 3s, this tree could often be mistaken for an oversized Flowering Dogwood. Unlike that species, the Tupelo is often found growing in swamps.

Staghorn Sumac is one of our showiest shrubs in the fall. The red berries steeped in water make a tangy lemonade substitute.

Staghorn Sumac
(Rhus typhina)

A common roadside shrub in much of our region, this species forms clonal thickets by putting up numerous root sprouts. It is easily identified by the velvety twigs (like a stag's horn in the velvet), its conspicuous cone-shaped clusters of hairy, red fruits, and the large compound leaves containing 19 or more long, pointed leaflets.

(opposite page)

A clone of Staghorn Sumac, originating by sprouts from a single root system.

Pollen-bearing male flower catkins of alders form in late summer and overwinter on the tree.

(opposite page)

Many forms of Rubus—brambles, blackberry, raspberry, and thimbleberry—fill the open places of our rural areas.

Speckled Alder
(Alnus rugosa)

Speckled Alder forms dense clonal thickets along the streams in our North Country. Its tiny seeds are borne in small, woody cones, and its leaves, which usually fall while still green, have doubly toothed margins.

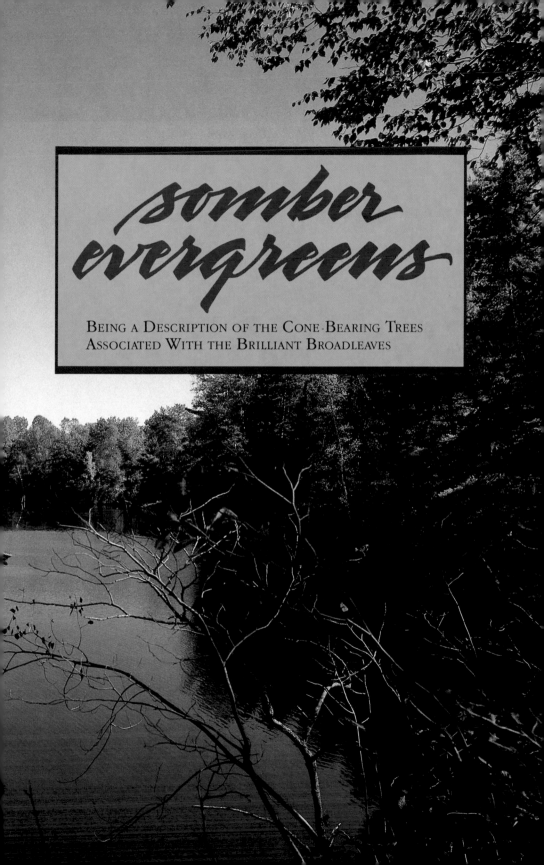

somber evergreens

BEING A DESCRIPTION OF THE CONE-BEARING TREES ASSOCIATED WITH THE BRILLIANT BROADLEAVES

Eastern White Pine
(Pinus strobus)

". . . our sylvan scenery owes the peculiar charm which distinguishes it from that of all other parts of the world to the wide-spreading dark green crowns of the White Pine, raised on stately shafts high above the level of the forest roof and breaking the monotony of its sky-line."

Thus did Charles Sprague Sargent pay tribute to "the most beautiful Pine-tree of eastern America" in his monumental *Silva of North America.* White Pine is the only eastern pine with needles clustered in 5s. These are "soft, slender, and delicate, three-sided, 3–4 inches long, light or dark bluish green, the inner side with a strong line of white bloom, producing a play of color when the wind stirs the branches," in the words of F. Schuyler Mathews. When young, its neatly geometric crown is supported by a trunk clothed in thin, smooth, greenish bark. In later years—and ages of 450 have been attained—the crown is shaggy in outline, made up of long, gracefully upswept branches arising on a cylindrical trunk covered with thick, furrowed bark, dark purplish-gray in cast. The great size of old-growth White Pines flabbergasted early settlers accustomed to Europe's unimpressive flora. Extravagant reports—or reports of extravagant trees: we will never know which—tell of a White Pine cut in 1736 near Dunstable, Massachusetts, with a seven-foot, eight-inch diameter at its butt end; one in Maine that was 6 feet in diameter and 240 feet tall; and a tree in Lincoln, New Hampshire, that was, according to a historian who "heard" this, 260 feet tall! Tall trees or tall tales, the awe in which White Pine was held is evident. Perhaps the tallest white pine still with us today is the "Grandmother Tree" of the Charles Lathrop Pack Demonstration Forest north of Warrensburg, New York. This 315-year-old survivor is about 4½ feet in diameter and soars 170 feet cloudwards.

White Pine bears its tiny winged seeds in cones that hang like clusters of green fingers in summer, and dry and open in the fall. The seeds germinate and grow to seedlings

(overleaf)

Eastern White Pines (center) in company with Red Pine, White Spruce, and Balsam Fir, illuminated by a blazing Red Maple.

(opposite page)

Eastern White Pine once provided the masts for Britain's navy.

Eastern White Pine is the only pine native to our region that has 5-needled clusters.

most readily when they are lightly covered with loamy soil. That is why White Pine stands often date back to the year a hurricane uprooted trees wholesale, causing mounds of soil to be brought up on their roots; or to the time an unproductive plowed field was abandoned. White Pines growing scattered among oaks and hickories often owe their establishment to gray squirrels whose digging—as they energetically buried acorns or hickory nuts—covered with bare soil White Pine seeds freshly fallen from their cones.

The Indians who preceded the early settlers made good use of these trees, however they became established.

126

White Pine provided them medicine and emergency food.
They boiled the needles to make tea that cured scurvy,
thanks to its high vitamin C content, and that soothed sore
throats. They used the aromatic resin to treat rheumatism,
burns, sores, and injuries. The inner bark tissue was
stripped in winter, or in spring when its sugar content was
at its peak, to be used as a foodstuff in lean years. Early
explorers in the Adirondacks, especially, came upon areas
where many pines had been stripped of bark. The name
Adirondack is from the Mohawk *Hatirongtaks*, literally
"they eat trees," and was applied to the Algonquian tribes
who had come from north of the St. Lawrence River. Early

*These resinous cones
of Eastern White Pine
shed their winged
seeds before they fall
from the tree.*

127

New Englanders went beyond the mere eating of trees: they developed a recipe for candying the tender spring shoots of White Pine.

The long straight trunks of White Pines, and their strength and relatively light weight, convinced the British Admiralty that divine intervention had assured a perpetual supply of naval mast-timber, a tremendously important strategic material in the days of sail. Mast traffic to Britain began in 1645. Starting in 1691, non-privately owned White Pines 24 inches or more in diameter a foot above ground level were reserved for the Royal Navy; and in 1719 the practice of blazing mast trees with the King's Broad Arrow was begun to discourage illicit cutting. This policy, and penalties imposed on violators, were among the irritations leading to the Revolutionary War. In Pennsylvania, White Pine masts 90 feet long and 40 inches at the butt were still being rafted down the Susquehanna rapids to Chesapeake Bay and the shipyards of Baltimore as late as 1860.

The commercial exploitation of White Pine began in Maine, and what happened there mirrors the fate of White Pine elsewhere. The first sawmills were built at York in 1623 and eleven years later at South Berwick. By 1675 fifty mills were sawing White Pine in great numbers, and by 1853 Henry David Thoreau could write of an encounter with a logging contractor in the woods near Moosehead Lake:

"I talked with one of them, telling him that I had come all this distance partly to see where the white-pine ... grew, but that on this and a previous excursion into another part of Maine I had found it a scarce tree; and I asked him where I must look for it. With a smile, he answered, that he could hardly tell me. However, he said that he had found enough to employ two teams the next winter in a place where there was thought to be none left. What was considered a 'tip-top' tree now was not looked at twenty years ago. ...." (The Maine Woods).

Thoreau also learned in Bangor of a White Pine containing 4500 board feet, and worth $90, for which a three-and-a-half-mile skid road had been built. Meanwhile, the White Pine industry was abandoning cut-out New England,

*Bald Eagles often nest
or perch in old White
Pines within a
quarter-mile of water.*

*The graceful feather
form of large Eastern
White Pines belies the
ruggedness of their
massive trunks.*

New York, and Pennsylvania, and moving west to the Lake States. Between 1849 and 1909 over *one hundred billion* board feet of White Pine was cut from the forests of Michigan alone, and in the 24 years from 1873 to 1897 one hundred and sixty-eight billion feet were cut in the three Lakes States. The same "reckless, inexcusable waste and inordinate cutting" was depleting the woods of Wisconsin, Minnesota, and southern Ontario from the mouth of the Ottawa River to Georgian Bay. In the peak year of 1899 White Pine production reached 9.4 billion board feet in the U.S. By the turn of the century Sargent lamented that "the great trees which were once the pride of the northern forest no longer exist" and most of the white pine cut was going into humble things like boxes and crates.

(opposite page)

The northern forest is a rich mixture of broadleaved and coniferous trees.

Since then, White Pine has made a remarkable comeback. In Maine, as throughout our region, White Pine, finally ignored as being of low commercial value, is again becoming important in the landscape, if not yet in lumber markets. Though they continue to be ravaged by the White Pine blister rust, and often made bushy by attacks of the White Pine weevil, White Pines are again raising dark green crowns on stately shafts, proving that our region can still grow giants.

Jack Pine
(Pinus banksiana)

Jack pine is the great coniferous weed of North America.
Over thousands of square miles in the Lake States, and
across a vast Canadian empire stretching from Nova Scotia
north and west into the Mackenzie River Valley, this little
pine covers plains and low hills shunned by most other
trees. It is rare in the northeastern states, but is found
locally in New York and Maine; and in New Hampshire,
where it reaches 2500 feet elevation in the White Mountains. Almost everywhere it grows, jack pine is found in
nearly pure stands, sometimes of great extent, on infertile
soils that are sandy, dry, and highly acidic. Jack Pines usually present a scraggly, unkempt appearance, with crooked
stems and very short yellowish green needles (to 2 inches
long; grouped in clusters of 2) on short, twisted limbs.
Jack Pines are usually short-lived, but an extreme age of
230 years has been recorded. Though it is today in demand
for the manufacture of pulpwood, posts, poles, and ties,
there was a time when Jack Pine was avoided by the su-
perstitious as a "witch-tree." Sargent reminds us

*"It is considered dangerous to those who pass within ten
feet of its limbs, the danger being greater for women
than for men; it is believed to poison the soil in which it
grows and to be fatal to cattle browsing near it; and if
any misfortune comes to a man who has one of these
trees on his land, or to his cattle, it must be burned
down with wood, which is piled around it, for the preju-
dice against it is so strong that no one possessed of this
belief would venture to cut down a (Jack) Pine."*

The most important event in the life of a Jack Pine forest
is fire. The species needs fire in order to shed its seeds,
and to avoid being shaded by trees less adaptable to burns.
Jack Pine's adaptation to fire is exquisite and precise. Over
most of its range Jack Pine's 1–2 inch long cones, smooth,
pointed, and sickle-shaped, remain closed on the tree for
many years. The scales that conceal the tiny seeds—which

(opposite page)

*Dense thickets of Jack
Pine often take over
on burned areas in
the northern part of
our region.*

run about 130,000 to the pound!—are bonded by a resin that must be heated to about 122°F before it will melt. When a hot ground fire at last burns its way into the forest, bonds melt, scales part, and seeds sequestered for many years in the tree crowns at last spin to seedbed earth. As many as two million seeds may fall on one acre of ash-covered ground, with several thousand fast-growing Jack Pines among the survivors.

For unknown reasons, Jack Pine stands in the northern part of Michigan's Lower Peninsula are the nursery of one of our rarest birds—the Kirtland's warbler. The warbler lives most of its life amid tropical surroundings in the Bahamas, but its nesting requirements are amazingly specific. Nests are constructed on the ground, beneath the limbs of Jack Pines about eight to twenty years of age that are within stands at least eighty acres in extent. The only known Kirtland's nesting area is on state land managed by Michigan's Department of Natural Resources, and on the Huron National Forest, managed by the U.S. Forest Service. Both agencies have committed themselves to the task of maintaining habitat for the rare warbler, mainly by controlled burning of older Jack Pine forests to provide a continuous supply of new young stands.

(overleaf)

Jack Pine's "serotinous" cones cannot release their seeds until the heat of fire opens them.

(opposite page)

Birches and maples bend under the weight of a downstream breeze.

Red Pine

(Pinus resinosa)

About 100 million years ago a pine markedly similar to today's Red Pine left fossil remains behind in southern Minnesota. Since then, Red Pine has responded to the comings and goings of great glacial ice sheets by retreating and reinvading as changing conditions permitted. It survived the most recent glaciation in an Appalachian refuge, then migrated west and north into its present range, and now is found throughout most of our region except Ohio. Because present-day populations are the offspring of a small band of ice-age survivors, there is little genetic variation in this inbred pine—the trees are, genetically, all much the same.

Erroneously called Norway Pine, for several alleged reasons, of which none are persuasive, this is an attractive species that reaches large size in its major growing areas of the northern Lake States, Ontario, and Quebec. It is distinguished from other pines of our region by its long, always paired needles (4–6 inches in length, vs. Jack Pine's

(opposite page)

Most of our great old Red Pines are gone, but many second-growth stands can be found in the Lake States.

Red Pine cones are round and smooth, the needles long and paired.

Conifer needles, like these of Red Pine, can conduct photosynthesis all year, adding to the trees' food reserves.

maximum of 2 inches), and the broad, thick, reddish plates of bark that clothe the trunks of mature trees. That thick bark is highly fire-resistant, allowing Red Pines to survive fires better than such neighbors as White Pine and numerous broad-leaved trees. Red Pines can therefore continue to live and cast their light, winged seeds on burns, and are indeed typical post-fire inhabitants of sandy and gravelly parts of our region.

During the heyday of White Pine logging in the late 1800s, Red Pine also felt the axe. Vast pineries of these two species in Michigan, Wisconsin, Minnesota, and Ontario were largely depleted of their virgin Red Pine, whose lumber was in demand for construction material.

Red Pine is not only useful, but is also easy to cultivate.

It does well in nurseries, is easily transplanted, grows rapidly, and—if planted on soils that do not become water-
logged—suffers relatively little from pests. It is therefore
a popular plantation species in our area, and is often grown
in large blocks of uniform-sized trees lined up with military precision.

It should not be confused with the Pitch Pine, which
has its needles in clusters of three. Pitch Pine becomes
fairly large—to 60 feet tall—in Pennsylvania, but elsewhere,
as in New England, the Albany "Pine Bush" and the New
Jersey "Pine Barrens," is usually a scraggly tree.

*(left) Porcupines eat
the nutritive inner
bark of many trees—
here a paper birch
provides practice for a
baby . . . (right) . . .
and here a conifer
faces death from the
girdling of its trunk.*

Balsam Fir

(Abies balsamea)

This is the only fir that grows wild in our region. Like the pines, spruces, and hemlock, firs are evergreen conifers. In common with spruces and hemlock, Balsam Fir has short needles attached singly to the branchlet, but they are flat, blunt, and aromatic, and they leave flat circular scars on the branchlet when they are removed. Unlike other conifers, Balsam Fir's cones develop only in the very top of the tree, and they are upright. They start to fall apart in the autumn, scale by scale, gradually releasing the seeds, so by next summer only a thin, spiky axis remains. Balsam fir is our most symmetrical tree, with a narrow spire-like crown made up of flat layers of dense, deep-green foliage. The smooth gray bark of young trees is punctuated by blisters containing a clear yellowish resin—Canada balsam—that was once used by Algonquins to treat burns, and more recently by the optical industry to cement lenses. The sticky resin and especially the needles of this tree exude a spicy fragrance that evokes the essence of the North Woods even long years after visiting there, and pillows stuffed with fir needles have long been a traditional souvenir of the region.

This species grows across the northern part of our area, but is absent from the southern parts of the Lake States, Ohio, much of Pennsylvania, Connecticut and Rhode Island. Its habitats run the gamut from low timbered swamps to the windswept tops of the Adirondack and White Mountains, spanning the elevation range from sea level to over 5000 feet. Firs were once common that stood over 100 feet tall, but now a 60-foot tree is "respectable." On mountaintops firs sometimes form windswept, shrubby thickets due to the low temperatures and severe winds. Balsam fir can grow in dense shade, yet it aggressively moves into open disturbed areas. On moist or boggy sites its lower limbs, if in prolonged contact with the ground, can strike roots and then turn upwards, forming a group of "chicks" around the larger "hen." Trees found with Balsam Fir include Red and Sugar Maples, Paper and Yellow Birches,

(opposite page)

The Balsam Fir is immediately identified by its spire-like tip.

143

Black, Red, and White Spruces, Tamarack, Aspen and Hemlock.

Balsam Fir suffers many afflictions, so it is short-lived, seldom attaining 200 years. Its most serious insect attackers are the spruce budworm, which devours its pollen cones and needles in the spring, and the balsam woolly aphid. The latter, a European insect first found in our forests in 1908, infests trunks, branches, and needles of firs. The tiny aphids, concealed under a mass of white ribbons of wax, suck sap from the inner bark and inject a saliva that causes the ends of twigs to swell. Growth ceases on heavily infested trees, and death soon follows. Balsam Fir forests high on mountains often die in "waves" that slowly move upslope. As the trees get taller and more exposed to the wind, their needles dry out; and their tender, young root tips are destroyed as the tree rocks back and forth during storms. But fir seedlings appear among the dead snags to establish a new generation of Balsam Fir, as the cycle is completed.

Crush Balsam Fir's flat needles and experience an unforgettable aroma.

Balsam Fir cones disintegrate in the fall, releasing their seeds to fly on the wind.

Eastern Hemlock
(*Tsuga canadensis*)

Campers know Hemlock as a species to avoid. Its branch knots are so hard they will chip an axe; and its wood will vigorously throw dangerous sparks when burned in the campfire. But it was not always spurned. Several early observers noted how Indians boiled and mashed Hemlock's inner bark to make a plaster for the treatment of sores and swellings. The lumber has always found a use in rough construction. And in the Nineteenth century, Hemlock bark was a primary source of tannin for the leather industry. It was common then for felled trees—the best of them to 160 feet tall with 6-foot diameters at the base—to be left in the woods to rot after the bark was stripped off; or for standing trees to be stripped, leaving vast numbers of dead woody snags to bleach in the sun. In New York State, the 1887 bark harvest was 1.2 million tons, but within 14 years the Forest, Fish and Game Commission reported of the Catskills that the tanning industry "... is now extinct in that region, the tanneries having been abandoned ... as the supply of bark became exhausted." Leather tanned with Hemlock bark had a red coloration, so oak bark was often put in the mix.

This lovely tree, distinguished by its dark trunk with purplish tones in the bark; short, flat needles, deep green to blue-green above with bright white stripes beneath arrayed in flat sprays; and drooping branch and leader tips, grows up in the dense shade of the forest and outlasts the other species it finally dominates. It is mixed singly or in small groves, among pines, firs, spruces, maples, cherry, and beech. At 20 to 30 years it starts producing tiny cones with winged seeds that are cast in the wind in the fall and germinate the next June. Seedlings often become established on moss, logs, or stumps. A sapling can grow almost imperceptibly for a century or more, and then with dramatic rapidity when the death of an overstory tree gives it a place in the sun. Hemlock's favored habitats are cool and rainy, with acidic soil. It occurs at sea level and to 2500 feet in mountain areas. Hemlock keeps well: trees

The last great nesting of the now-extinct passenger pigeon in New York State was in 1868, when millions of birds invaded a forest in Allegheny County along the Pennsylvania border. Many of the Hemlocks are said to have held 30 to 40 nests.

(opposite page)

Eastern Hemlock can be distinguished from our other native conifers by its small, pendent cones and short, flat needles.

500–600 years old were not uncommon, and one is said to have reached 988 years, perhaps the oldest tree in northeastern North America.

In the winter, porcupines cut many branchlets from Hemlocks, feed on the needles of the year, and discard the rest. When these fall to the ground, they become a windfall for families of white-tailed deer, which often "yard up" in Hemlock groves.

In the last century, many large hemlocks were felled and their bark used in tanning leather.

(opposite page)

Eastern Hemlock has been known to live over 900 years.

White Spruce (center) often grows with the spire-like Balsam Fir.

White Spruce
(Picea glauca)

Spruces are the only needle-leaved trees in our region that have almost-square needles that can be rolled between thumb and forefinger. Fir and Hemlock are flat-needled, and cannot be rolled. When spruce needles are plucked or fall from the twig, they leave behind prominent, raised, woody leaf-bases; and these make leafless spruce branches coarse and rasp-like to the touch. Firs leave flat, circular scars on the twig, and Hemlock has tiny, raised leaf-bases.

White Spruce has needles that emit a "powerful polecat odor." As a result, it has also been called Cat Spruce and Skunk Spruce. It is the only native conifer in our region whose smell is offensive rather than aromatic. It is not a tree that is restricted to our region, but is the most widely distributed cone-bearer of North America, growing along blue water in Newfoundland as well as in Alaska. It even ascends the Rockies of northwestern Montana where it hybridizes with one of the western spruces. White Spruce is our most important pulpwood species, and it provides the newsprint for many a daily newspaper. Like other spruces,

When White Spruce cones mature in the fall, the scales part, allowing the winged seeds to flutter to the ground.

Throughout its broad range, White Spruce provides seeds rich in protein and fats for the Red Squirrel.

it also yields light, creamy lumber suitable for many uses, including the sound boards of musical instruments. Although it is common in our region, where the climate is relatively mild, White Spruce has apparently attained its greatest height (over 180 feet) and age (500 years) in western Canada. It survives the rigors of the far north where, according to Sargent: ". . . its stems choke the mouths of every arctic American river, strewing the adjacent shores with heaps of driftwood and testifying to its abundance on their shifting banks." In our region it is often associated

Boiled White Spruce shoots were used in brewing the anti-scurvy preparation, "spruce beer."

153

with Quaking Aspen, Red and Black Spruces, Balsam Fir, Tamarack, and White Pine.

White Spruce was the first North American spruce, and one of the first trees, to be mentioned in publication. Jacques Cartier noted seeing it along the Saguenay River in Southeastern Quebec in his *Bref Recit et Succincte Narration de la Navigation Faite in MDXXXV* (1535). Among the Indians, white spruce was the source of *wattap*, or *watape*—pliable roots used for general cordage, for weaving baskets, and for lacing birch-bark seams. Ernest Thompson Seton recommended soaking wattap for an hour in hot water to soften it, removing the bark, and scrubbing it smooth. He dyed wattap red with squaw-berries, black with extracts of Smooth Sumac or Butternut bark, orange with inner-bark decoctions of Alder or Sassafras, or dull red by soaking it in "strong tea" from the pink inner bark of Hemlock. White Spruce was also a source of "spruce beer," a scurvy remedy made by boiling young green shoots, adding maple sugar or honey, and allowing to ferment. One must assume that suffering from scurvy was considered a worse fate than drinking spruce beer. Treatment of scurvy is discussed further under Northern White-Cedar.

Red Spruce
(Picea rubens)

Whoever hikes summer trails high in the Adirondack, Green, or White Mountains, the Laurentian Hills, or on the slopes of Katahdin, can hardly fail to be energized by the spicy-resinous scent of aromatic oils escaping the needles of Red Spruce, and its companion, Balsam Fir. This narrow-crowned conifer, its branches clothed in glossy, deep-yellow-green foliage, covers the high ridges (to 4,500 feet) of the eastern part of our region from Maine to Pennsylvania, and spreads widely at lower elevations from southern Quebec to Nova Scotia. In the mountains above 3000 feet its crowns pierce the cover of low clouds, milking them of moisture beyond what falls as rain and snow. Red Spruce mingles with birches, aspens, and maples, and drops to sea level on the Atlantic shores of Maine and Nova Scotia.

Like all spruces, this tree has wood that is long-fibered and strong for its weight—therefore useful for lumber or wood pulp. As a result, many once-great forests of Red Spruce have felt the axe, from early settlement to the present day.

Red Spruce are not exceptionally large: trees in old-growth forests seldom exceed 75 feet in height and 2 feet in diameter, though a record exists of a 162-foot tall tree from the southern Appalachians. One must therefore question the tree-identification prowess of John Josselyn, as quoted by the dendrologist Charles Sprague Sargent. According to Sargent, Josselyn wrote in his *New England's Rarities Discovered: In Birds, Beasts, Fishes, Serpents, and Plants of That Country* (1672) that:

"Spruce is a goodly tree, of which they make Masts for Ships, and Sail Yards. It is generally conceived by those that have skill in Building of Ships, that here is absolutely the best Trees in the World, many of them being three Fathom about, and of great length."

"Three Fathom about" would mean roughly six feet in diameter, suspiciously large for any of our region's spruces. Josselyn is further quoted from his *An Account of Two Voyages to New England*:

"At Pascataway *there is now a Spruce-tree, brought down to the water-side by our Mass-men, of an incredible bigness, and so long that no Skipper durst ever yet adventure to ship it, but there it lyes and Rots."*

Again, that does not sound at all like a spruce. This author would guess that in both cases Josselyn was referring to White Pines, which, as we have already seen, were reported to attain enormous sizes; and which were the premier mast-trees. In past centuries the distinctions between pines, spruces, and firs were not as clearly drawn as they are today.

Today, Red Spruce has more than axes to take it to the brink. In addition to the usual assortment of mortality factors all trees must cope with—fire, wind, insects, disease— Red Spruce, like the canary in a coal mine, is showing the symptoms of life in a contaminated atmosphere. From North Carolina to Vermont's Camel's Hump, Red Spruces are dying in alarming numbers. Research has shown the likely, but not yet certain, cause to be acidified rain and snow falling through polluted air: the same toxin that has turned a fourth of Adirondack lakes to weak vinegar. Even on the Maine coast, acidified fog and elevated levels of ozone cause death of green needles. If Red Spruce continues to die back in large numbers, like its European relative, the Norway Spruce, some of our region's great beauty spots will lose their distinctive character.

Distinguish Red Spruce from White Spruce by its fine-haired, reddish twigs, and reddish cones with rounded, smooth-edged scales. Distinguish it from Black Spruce by its yellowish, not bluish, foliage.

The rapid decline of Red Spruce, believed due to acid rain, has caused serious concern.

Black Spruce

(Picea mariana)

Black Spruce is the typical conifer of the subarctic zone where the northern edge of the boreal forest is interfingered with the southern edge of the tundra. Here it grows very slowly, sometimes taking a century to attain a stem diameter of one inch. But in our region Black Spruce grows more rapidly, and in Canada's Maritime Provinces it is the most commonly planted tree, with over 35 million seedlings a year devoted to the future pulpwood harvest. Black Spruce often dwells in muskegs—shallow ponds in the process of being filled by floating mats of sphagnum moss. It is also found in drier uplands mixed with Balsam Fir, Tamarack, White Spruce, Paper Birch, Red Maple, and Quaking Aspen.

Black Spruce has interesting strategies for reproducing itself. In the far north, its cones remain closed, and a tree may accumulate 20 years worth of cones with healthy seeds inside. Then, when a fire burns the muskeg vegetation, its heat opens the cones, allowing Black Spruce to dump thousands of seeds on the nutrient-rich ashes, where they can quickly become established ahead of other species. No other spruce is known to take advantage of fire in this way, though several pines do so. In our region, seeds are apparently not retained as long, and are shed from their cones mainly in late winter and early spring. The lower limbs of Black Spruces often die, decay, and fall from the tree, leaving ". . . dense tufts of dark branches like plumes upon poles (which) present a strange spectacle to the traveler who for the first time crosses the larger muskegs, especially at twilight, for he seems to be looking over a weird procession, stretching often mile after mile until lost in the distance." It is in these tuft-like crowns that the masses of cones are found. The seeds in those cones are an important food resource to white-winged crossbills. These small forest birds eat the seeds of Tamarack and White Spruce in the fall, but as these become depleted they switch to Black Spruce in order to get through the winter. All conifers have highly nutritive seeds amply provided

(opposite page)
Black Spruce characterizes the bog forest of the far North Woods.

(overleaf)
The variety of species of the northern hardwood forests produces a fall mosaic.

161

A Black Spruce bog in the far north.

(opposite page)

Black Spruce and Tamarack often share the same bogs and river bottoms.

with protein, and often heavy with energy-giving fats as well. White-winged crossbills do not necessarily have an easy time extracting Black Spruce seeds—Black Spruce cone scales are quite thick and tough, so it takes some effort to feed from cones not yet fully opened. A Black Spruce branch in prolonged contact with wet ground can put out roots, and turn its new growth upwards, mimicking a tree. Circles of such rooted branches—or "layers"—form clones around the parent tree.

Identify Black Spruce by its masses of old cones still clinging to the branches, close to the trunk. Distinguish it from Red Spruce by its blue-green foliage, and from white spruce by the pleasant aroma of its crushed needles.

162

Eastern red-cedar invades open areas where flying birds have excreted its seeds.

Eastern Red-Cedar
(*Juniperus virginiana*)

Eastern Red-Cedar is, despite its name, a juniper. And junipers, despite their berry-like fruits, are conifers: for arcane reasons, those little blue berries are technically cones. (Compromise science and common sense and call them berry-cones.) Crush a berry-cone, and inhale the volatile oil that gives gin its essence. To associate "gin" with "juniper" or *"genévrier"* is to appreciate simultaneously how our language evolves, and how plants contribute to our material culture. This juniper has contributed much else. Oil of red cedar, distilled from its wood—especially old stumps—is used in the manufacture of perfumes, soap, polishes, and moth repellent. Moths are supposedly repelled by the odors emanating from the rose-red heartwood, as owners of cedar chests believe. And pencils were at one time on this continent made almost entirely from this tree's wood. Until, that is, the buyers of pencil timber depleted the largest groves of red-cedar, and purchased all the old cedar cabins, floorboards, and rail fences they could find, before heading West for California's virgin forests of Incense-cedar.

Of course the Indians were the first to know of Eastern Red-Cedar's virtues, especially its medicinal properties. They crushed the berries and spread the oil on their skin as an insect repellent. They chewed the berry-cones to treat headache. They inhaled the smoke of burning twigs to cure head colds and coughs, and treated ailments as varied as dysentery and rheumatism with red-cedar preparations.

Eastern Red-Cedar is an evergreen conifer with tiny scale-like leaves pressed to the surface of the branchlet. It is common in the southern parts of our region, but absent from the northern Lake States, most of Maine, and points east. It is frequently found growing on thin, rocky, limestone soils. Large trees are very rare, but before the 19th Century heyday of the cedar pencil, specimens more than a hundred feet in height seem to have been common.

Eastern Red-Cedar is an extremely variable tree, and it

Eastern Red Cedar

The Cedar Waxwing is named for the tree whose fruit it prefers— the red-cedar.

can be easily propagated by the rooting of branch cuttings
which can then be planted outdoors. As a result there are
many cultivated varieties of this species grown for ornamental uses: some conical, some columnar, some spreading or globose in form.

The masses of ripe blue berry-cones are attractive not
only to gardeners, but to our birds as well. Junipers have
long been known to depend on birds to spread their seeds.
A recent study has shed light on the details of Eastern Red-
Cedar's relationship with a group of fruit-eating birds. Individual trees can bear enormous numbers of berry-cones-
up to three million, or more. These ripen in late summer
through October, but they stay tightly attached to the tree
until next spring. Thus they are "on display" to the birds
that seek them for half the year. Some of the berry-cone
consumers are birds that forage alone, like yellow-rumped
(myrtle) warblers, eastern bluebirds, and downy woodpeckers. They account for a slow but steady removal of
ripe fruits throughout the fall and winter. But the flock-
feeders—the cedar waxwings, European starlings, and robins—descend upon the cedars and strip whole crops from
them in bouts of frantic feeding. Now, this much was
known even in the early days of the American republic,
and will surprise no one who has read William Bartram's
Travels, published in 1791. According to Bartram, writing
of the "cedar bird":

*"The longest period of their appearance in Pennsylva-
nia is in the spring and first of June, at the time the
early cherries are ripe, when they are numerous; and
in the autumn when the Cedar berries are ripe (Junipe-
rus americana) they arrive in large flights, and with the
robins (Turdus migratorius) and yellow rump (Parus
cedrus) soon strip those trees of their berries, after which
they disappear again. . . ."*

After digesting the fleshy berry-cone material, all these
birds excrete the seeds, either randomly while in flight,
or from perches. Passage through a bird's digestive tract
increases the seed's ability to germinate, presumably because stomach acids soften the bony seed coat. By dis-
persing seeds into abandoned pasturelands, birds that feed

The blue berry-cones of Eastern Red-cedar are an attractive food to migratory birds.

upon Eastern Red-Cedar berry-cones have been establishing new groves of cedars that will provide many millions of new berry-cones for birds of the future. If the millions of new cedars becoming established are let alone for a century or more, giants may again raise their compact green crowns against the sky.

*The dark crowns of
our conifers contrast
pleasingly with the
brilliant broadleaved
trees.*

Northern White-Cedar
(Thuja occidentalis)

The Northern White-Cedar, or Arborvitae, is common in the northern parts of our region. It grows both on uplands, especially lands underlain by limestone; and in moist places like riverbanks, lakeshores, and swamps that have thin, well-decomposed peat. It grows less far into bogs than its associates Black Spruce and Tamarack. Other neighbors include Red Spruce, Sugar and Red Maples, Balsam Fir, Hemlock, Aspen and White Pine.

Arborvitae is usually a small tree—a maximum height of just 80 feet has been reported—with a conical crown that extends to the ground on trees growing in the open. It has shallow roots, and frequently blows down; when it does so in moist soils, branches lying in contact with the ground may root, and turn upwards at the tip to mimic a normal tree. Its foliage consists of tiny paired scale-leaves pressed to the twig and lying elegantly in flat, lacy sprays, unlike any other native tree in our region. The scale-leaves each have a small gland that contains cells from which an aromatic essential oil is secreted. Thus crushed Arborvitae foliage provides perhaps the greatest olfactory thrill to be found in our forests. Indians inhabiting our region used crushed foliage as a poultice for reducing swellings, and, steeped in boiling water, for treating chest pain. To cure coughs and to "purify" the blood, they drank a tea brewed from the leaves. White settlers adopted the use of "cedar tea" but Henry David Thoreau found it too medicinal for his palate, despite claims it would cure gout, fever, catarrh, dropsy, and warts. Perhaps Thoreau would have found less objectionable the common practice of making a paste of boiled foliage and bear grease, for applying to rheumatic joints.

Cedar tea is rich in vitamin C—as is probably true of all tree leaves—but because Arborvitae is evergreen, the tea can be made any time of year. It is conjectured that on one of Jacques Cartier's voyages to Canada, in the 1530s, twenty-five of his men died of scurvy, and that Indians along the St. Charles River informed Cartier of the curative

(opposite page)

The bark of the Northern White-cedar, or Arborvitae, was used by Indians for cordage.

White-tailed deer frequently take shelter in Arborvitae thickets, and heavily browse the nutritious foliage.

powers of "Annedda," an evergreen decoction of White-Cedar. Therewith, Captain Cartier brought home with him seedlings of this wonderful tree, which France's King Francis I dubbed *"l'arbre de vie"*—tree of life—later Latinized to Arborvitae. Embedded in this tale, which includes contributions by John Ray and Francis Parkman, is the claim that White Cedar was among the first North American trees brought to Europe. But the story becomes more complicated with the botanist Rafinesque's claim that White Spruce was implicated in the sailors' cure.

The aromatic wood of this charming tree is soft, weak, durable, and very light in weight. Thus it has found favor over the years for canoe frames, shingles, poles, and posts. The trunk is covered by a thin layer of shreddy bark that once was used in cordage.

Though the foliage of Arborvitae is good moose feed, and the little seeds are eaten by red squirrels, crossbills, and pine siskins, it is the white-tailed deer that one most closely associates with this tree. Ernest Thompson Seton has caught the essence of that relationship:

(overleaf)
Arborvitae foliage may have saved the life of sixteenth-century sailors.

"*. . . White Cedar is noted for the dense thickets it forms in the hollows and hillsides of the eastern Canadian region. These banks, like evergreen hedges, are so close that they greatly modify the winter climate within their bounds—outside there may be a raging blizzard that no creature can face, while within all is dead calm and the frost less intense. The Cedar feeds its proteges too, for its evergreen boughs and abundant nuts are nutrient food despite their rosin smell and taste. Never do the deer and hares winter better than in cedar cover, and if there is (a) great thicket in their region, they surely gather there as sparrows at a barn, or as rats around a brewery.*"

A Northern White-cedar thicket surrounded by birches, firs, spruces, and maples.

175

Scientific Names of Trees Mentioned in Text

Alder, Speckled	*Alnus rugosa*
Arborvitae	*Thuja occidentalis*
Ash, Black	*Fraxinus nigra*
Ash, Red	*Fraxinus pennsylvanica*
Ash, White	*Fraxinus americana*
Aspen, Bigtooth	*Populus grandidentata*
Aspen, Quaking	*Populus tremuloides*
Basswood	*Tilia americana*
Beech, American	*Fagus grandifolia*
Birch, Bog	*Betula pumila*
Birch, Gray	*Betula populifolia*
Birch, Paper	*Betula papyrifera*
Birch, River	*Betula nigra*
Birch, Sweet	*Betula lenta*
Birch, Yellow	*Betula alleghaniensis*
Boxelder	*Acer negundo*
Butternut	*Juglans cinerea*
Cherry, Black	*Prunus serotina*
Cherry, Fire	*Prunus pensylvanica*
Chokecherry	*Prunus virginiana*
Cottonwood, Eastern	*Populus deltoides*
Dogwood, Flowering	*Cornus florida*
Dogwood, Red-Osier	*Cornus stolonifera*
Elm, American	*Ulmus americana*
Elm, Rock	*Ulmus thomasii*
Elm, Slippery	*Ulmus rubra*
Fir, Balsam	*Abies balsamea*
Hackberry	*Celtis occidentalis*
Hawthorn	*Crataegus* species
Hemlock, Eastern	*Tsuga canadensis*
Hickory, Bitternut	*Carya cordiformis*
Hickory, Mockernut	*Carya tomentosa*
Hickory, Pignut	*Carya glabra*
Hickory, Shagbark	*Carya ovata*
Hickory, Shellbark	*Carya laciniosa*
Larch, Western	*Larix occidentalis*
Maple, Black	*Acer nigrum*
Maple, Red	*Acer rubrum*
Maple, Silver	*Acer saccharinum*
Maple, Sugar	*Acer saccharum*
Mountain-ash, American	*Sorbus americana*
Mulberry, Red	*Morus rubra*
Oak, Black	*Quercus velutina*
Oak, Bur	*Quercus macrocarpa*
Oak, Northern Red	*Quercus rubra*

Oak, Pin	*Quercus palustris*
Oak, Scarlet	*Quercus coccinea*
Oak, Shumard	*Quercus shumardii*
Oak, Swamp White	*Quercus bicolor*
Oak, White	*Quercus alba*
Pine, Eastern White	*Pinus strobus*
Pine, Jack	*Pinus banksiana*
Pine, Pitch	*Pinus rigida*
Pine, Red	*Pinus resinosa*
Poplar, Balsam	*Populus balsamifera*
Red-Cedar, Eastern	*Juniperus virginiana*
Sassafras	*Sassafras albidum*
Spruce, Black	*Picea mariana*
Spruce, Red	*Picea rubens*
Spruce, White	*Picea glauca*
Sumac, Smooth	*Rhus glabra*
Sumac, Staghorn	*Rhus typhina*
Sycamore	*Platanus occidentalis*
Tamarack	*Larix laricina*
Tupelo, Black	*Nyssa sylvatica*
Walnut, Black	*Juglans nigra*
White-Cedar, Northern	*Thuja occidentalis*
Willow, Bebb's	*Salix bebbiana*
Willow, Black	*Salix nigra*
Willow, Peachleaf	*Salix amygdaloides*
Willow, Pussy	*Salix discolor*
Willow, Shining	*Salix lucida*

For Further Reference

Barnes, Burton V. and Warren H. Wagner, Jr. Michigan Trees, a Guide to the Trees of Michigan and the Great Lakes Region. University of Michigan Press, Ann Arbor. 1981.

Brooks, Karl L. A Catskill Flora and Economic Botany, II. *Coniferales.* New York State Museum Bull. 441, Albany, NY. 1980.

Brooks, Karl L. A Catskill Flora and Economic Botany, III. *Apetalae.* New York State Museum Bull. 443, Albany, NY. 1980.

Edlin, Herbert L. Trees and Man. Columbia University Press, New York. 1976.

Harlow, William M. Trees of the Eastern United States and Canada. McGraw-Hill, New York. 1942.

Hosie, R. C. Native Trees of Canada, 7th Edition. Canadian Forest Service, Ottawa. 1969.

Little, Elbert L., Jr. The Audubon Society Field Guide to North American Trees, Eastern Region. Alfred A. Knopf, Inc., New York. 1980.

Nearing, Helen and Scott Nearing. The Maple Sugar Book. John Day, New York. 1950.

Peattie, Donald Culross. A Natural History of Trees of Eastern and Central North America, 2nd Edition. Houghton-Mifflin Co., Boston. 1966.

Pielou, E. C. The World of Northern Evergreens. Cornell University Press, Ithaca, New York. 1988.

Rowe, J. S. Forest Regions of Canada. Canad. Forestry Service Publ. 1300, Ottawa. 1972.

Sloane, Eric. A Reverence for Wood. Ballantine Books, New York. 1973.

(opposite page)

Raspberry leaves prepare to "fall from giving shade above, to make one texture of faded brown. . . ."

Index

A

Abscisin, 6
Acid rain, 24, 156
Acorn
  Burr Oak, 82
  Northern Red Oak, 87, 89
  White Oak, 81–82
Alder, 6, 74, 107, 154
  Speckled, **43**, 120, **120**
Allelopathic effect, 76–77
Anthocyanidin, 5–6
Anthocyanin, 5–7, 13–14
Aphid, balsam woolly, 144
Arabinogalactan, 109
Arborvitae. *See* White-Cedar, Northern
Ash, 6, 52, 64
  Black, 91–94, 104, 107
  Green. *See* Ash, Red
  Red, 37, 45, 94
  White, 19, 76, **90**, 91–94, **92–94**, 99
Aspen, 13, 45, 57, 144, 155, 171
  Bigtooth, 70
  Quaking, 7, **31**, **60–61**, 64, **66**, 67–70, **68–71**, 153, 161
  Trembling. *See* Aspen, Quaking
Auxin, 6

B

Balsam, 73
  Canada, 143
Bark, birch, 49
Basswood, 19, 29, 37, 64, 76, **98**, 99–101, **100**, 104
Bear, black, 41, 82, **87**
Beaver, 35, 52, 70, **70**, 109
Beech, 5, 19, 29, 57, 76, 91, 147
  American, **40**, 41–43
Beetle, elm bark, 104
Birch, 6, 15, **141**, 155
  Bog, 107
  Gray, 52, 64
  Paper, 19, **48**, 49–52, **50–51**, **53**, 74, **101**, 143, 161
  River, 37, 45
  Silver. *See* Birch, Yellow
  Sweet, 57
  Yellow, 19, 29, 41, **56**, 57–59, **58**, 91, 99, 143
Blackberry, **121**
Black knot disease, Black Cherry, 64

Blister rust, White Pine, 130
Bluebird, eastern, 167
Boxelder, 37, 45
Bud, winter, 13
Budworm, spruce, 144
Butternut, 77, 154

C

Canker, Butternut, 77
Carotene, 4, 6, 14
Carotenoid, 4–7
Casebearer, larch, 109
Caterpillar, tent, 24, 64
Catkin, 45, 52, 57, 74
Cherry, 13, 15, 147
  Black, 19, 57, **62**, 63–64, **65**, 91, 99
  Cabinet. *See* Cherry, Black
  Fire, 64
  Pin. *See* Cherry, Fire
  Rum. *See* Cherry, Black
Chlorophyll, 3–7
Chloroplast, 4
Chokecherry, 64
Chromoplast, 4
Clone, 67
Cone
  Balsam Fir, 144
  Black Spruce, 161–62
  Eastern Hemlock, 147
  Jack Pine, 133–36
  Red-Cedar, 165, 167–68
  White Pine, 125–29
Cottonwood, 6, 37, 45, 74
  Eastern, 45, **73**, 74, 104
Crossbill, 175
  white-winged, 161–62

D

Deer, white-tailed, 31, 41, 52, 96, 148, 169, 175
Dogwood, 91
  Flowering, 13, 114
  Red-Osier, 114, **114**
Duck, wood, 81–82
Dutch elm disease, 102, 104

E

Eagle, bald, **129**
Elm, 15, 64
  American, 37, 45, 99, **102**, 103–105, **105**
  Rock, 105
  Slippery, 105
  White. *See* Elm, American

F

Fall color hotline, 10–12
Fall festivals, 9
Finch, purple, **94**

Fir, 52, 147, 150
  Balsam, 29, 52, 57, 74, 107, **142**, 143–44, **144–45**, 154–55, **158–59**, 161, 171
Forcing, 13
Fox, 115
  eastern red, **65**

G

Grackle, purple, 82
Grosbeak, 31
  evening, **36**
Grouse, 41, 52
  ruffed, 70, 82, 87

H

Hackberry, 37, 117, **117**
Hardwood forest, mixed, **8**
Hare, snowshoe, 70
Hawk, red-tailed, 20
Hawthorn, **114**, 115
Hemlock, 19, 29, 57, 64, 91, 99, 143–44, 150, 154, 171
  Eastern, **146–49**, 147–48
Hickory, 6, 76, 89, 91, 126
  Bitternut, 37
  Mockernut, 97
  Pignut, 97
  Shagbark, 95–97, **95**, **97**
  Shellbark, 97
Honeybee, 99
Hormone, 6
Horsechestnut, 13
Hotline telephone number, 10–12

I

Insect, leaf-eating, 15, **15**

J

Jay, 100
  blue, **42**, 41–42
Juglone, 76–77
Juniper, 165, 167

K

Kingfisher, **73**

L

Linden, American. *See* Basswood
Locust, Black, 6

M

Maple, 5, 52, 64, 91, 147, 155
  Creek. *See* Maple, Silver